THEMATIC UNIT
TIDE POOLS
and CORAL REEFS

Written by Jeanne King
Edited by Patricia Miriani Sima
Illustrated by Cheryl Buhler

2005

Happy
8th
Birthday
Austin

your friends
Nabin, Neelee, Al

Teacher Created Materials, Inc.
6421 Industry Way
Westminster, CA 92683
www.teachercreated.com
©1993 Teacher Created Materials, Inc.
Reprinted, 2001
Made in U.S.A.
ISBN-1-55734-249-X

Table of Contents

Introduction

Tide Pools and Coral Reefs contains a captivating whole language thematic unit. Its 80 exciting pages are filled with a wide variety of lesson ideas and activities designed for use with primary children. At its core are two high-quality children's literature selections, *A House For Hermit Crab* and *At Home in the Coral Reef.* For each of these books, activities are included which set the stage for reading, encourage the enjoyment of the book, and extend the concepts gained. In addition, the theme is connected to the curriculum with activities in language arts, math, science, social studies, art, music, and life skills. Many of these activities encourage cooperative learning. Suggestions and patterns for games and ideas for a bulletin board are additional time savers for the busy teacher. Furthermore, directions are provided for a culminating activity that allows the students to produce products that can be shared beyond the classroom. All of these activities combine to make this book a very complete teacher resource.

This thematic unit includes the following:

- ❑ **literature selections**—summaries of two children's books with related lessons (complete with reproducible pages) that cross the curriculum

- ❑ **poetry**—suggested selections and lessons enabling students to write and publish their own works

- ❑ **planning guides**—suggestions for sequencing lessons each day of the unit

- ❑ **writing ideas**—daily suggestions as well as writing activities across the curriculum, including Big Books

- ❑ **curriculum connections**—in language arts, math, science, social studies, art, music, and life skills such as cooking and physical education

- ❑ **bulletin board ideas**—suggestions and plans for student-created and/or interactive bulletin boards

- ❑ **group projects**—to foster cooperative learning

- ❑ **a culminating activity**—which requires students to synthesize their learning to produce a product or engage in an activity that can be shared with others

- ❑ **a bibliography**—suggesting additional fiction and nonfiction books on the theme

To keep this valuable resource intact so that it can be used year after year, you may wish to punch holes in the pages and store them in a three-ring binder.

Introduction *(cont.)*

Why Whole Language?

A whole language approach involves children in using all modes of communication: reading, writing, listening, observing, illustrating, experiencing, and doing. Communication skills are interconnected and integrated into lessons that emphasize the whole of language rather than isolating its parts. The lessons revolve around selected literature. Reading is not taught as a separate subject from writing and spelling, for example. A child reads, writes (spelling appropriately for his/her level), speaks, listens, etc., in response to a literature experience introduced by the teacher. In this way, language skills grow naturally, stimulated by involvement and interest in the topic at hand.

Why Thematic Planning?

One very useful tool for implementing an integrated whole language program is thematic planning. By choosing a theme with correlative literature selections for a unit of study, a teacher can plan activities throughout the day that lead to a cohesive, in-depth study of the topic. Students will be practicing and applying their skills in meaningful contexts. Consequently, they will tend to learn and retain more. Both teachers and students will be freed from a day that is broken into unrelated segments of isolated drill and practice.

Why Cooperative Learning?

Besides academic skills and content, students need to learn social skills. No longer can this area of development be taken for granted. Students must learn to work cooperatively in groups in order to function well in modern society. Group activities should be a regular part of school life, and teachers should consciously include social objectives as well as academic objectives in their planning. For example, a group working together to write a report may need to select a leader. The teacher should make clear to the students and monitor the qualities of good leader-follower group interaction just as he/she would state and monitor the academic goals of the project.

Why Big Books?

An excellent cooperative, whole language activity is the production of Big Books. Groups of students or the whole class can apply their language skills, content knowledge, and creativity to produce a Big Book that can become a part of the classroom library to be read and reread. These books make excellent culminating projects for sharing beyond the classroom with parents, librarians, other classes, etc. Big Books can be produced in many ways and this thematic unit book includes directions for at least one method you may choose.

A House for Hermit Crab

by Eric Carle

Hermit Crab keeps outgrowing things. When he outgrows his first shell house, he is a little scared. The next one is large enough for him, "but it looks so—well, so plain." To his delight, all sorts of undersea creatures befriend him and agree to decorate and protect his home. Soon, Hermit Crab's new house is perfect but, unfortunately, Hermit Crab has now outgrown this home, too. Hermit Crab must move on again, but this time he is less scared. Though sad to leave all his friends, he looks forward to his new future as one with many exciting possibilities. Children will relate to this story, which shows that growing up, though sometimes frightening, can be fun and exciting.

Sample Plan

Day 1

- Use the Daily Writing Topics. (page 45)
- Distribute Things to Look for in a Tide Pool Checklist. (pages 9-11)
- Classify Shells.
- Measure Crabwalking in Centimeters. (page 50)

Day 2

- Continue Daily Writing Topics. (page 45)
- Complete I'm a Crustacean handout. (page 12)
- Read *A House for Hermit Crab*.
- Make a Paper Plate Crab. (page 70)

Day 3

- Continue Daily Writing Topics. (page 45)
- Respond to Poetry. (page 19)
- Begin Brine Shrimp Experiment. (page 22)
- Do *Hermit Crab* Readers' Theater. (pages 13-16)
- Graph Your Favorite Tide Pool Animal. (page 49)

Day 4

- Continue Daily Writing Topics. (page 45)
- Work on Marine Math. (page 21)
- Read Ralph's Narrow Escape. (pages 17-18)
- Do an Art Project. (pages 69-71)
- Sing Songs. (see page 73)

Day 5

- Continue Daily Writing Topics. (page 45)
- Respond to Poetry. (pages 19-20)
- Observe Brine Shrimp.
- Make Fingerprint Tide Pools. (page 70)
- Float an Egg Experiment. (page 53)

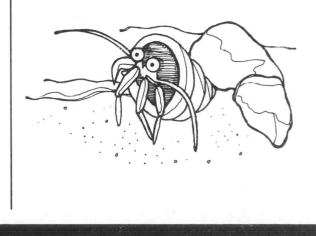

Overview of Activities

SETTING THE STAGE

1. Open the discussion by asking the students if they have ever made a big change in their lives, such as attending a new school, moving to a new home, or changing grade levels. What feelings did they experience when they found out about the move and when they made the move? How did their feelings change with time?

2. Pass out a variety of sea shells and coral to the class. Allow ample time for free exploration. When enough time has passed, explain that each of these shells was once a home for an animal. What kinds of animals do they believe once inhabited these shells? Ask the children to group the shells in different ways. Most will choose size, color, and shape, so encourage the children to try as many additional ways as possible. After they have explored many possibilities, brainstorm on the board the many different groupings. Have the students pick out the shells that also provide homes for a very special animal called the hermit crab found in the tide pools. The hermit crab is not like other crabs in that he has to "borrow" his shells from other animals as he grows, while other crabs simply grow shells.

3. Most pet stores sell inexpensive and easy-to-care-for hermit crabs. Bring one in to share with the class. These are shy, timid creatures which may be coaxed out more easily in a darkened, quiet room. The students may have to wait a few minutes for him to peek out, but the wait is well worth it.

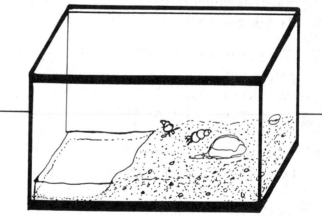

4. Read "I'm a Crustacean" on page 12. Write about finding a new home. Have the children share their own stories or write a class story.

5. Read about the tides and do the Reading a Tide Table handout on page 56.

ENJOYING THE BOOK

1. Read *A House for Hermit Crab* to the class. Discuss the main ideas in the story. How did Hermit Crab feel about the changes in his life at the beginning of the story? What types of things did he do to ease the tension of moving? Have you ever had a friend help you adjust to changes you have experienced? How did that help you? By the end of the book, what inside and outside changes did Hermit Crab experience?

Overview of Activities *(cont.)*

ENJOYING THE BOOK *(cont.)*

2. Introduce the Things to Look for in a Tide Pool Checklist (pages 9-11). Discuss the different characteristics of each animal. Ask children, "If these animals could talk, what voices might they use?" Have children experiment with a variety of expressions and voices with each other by introducing themselves to the class or to a partner as one of these animals.

3. Reread the story as a Readers' Theater (pages 13-16). Encourage children to try their new voices and use a variety of expressions in their acting. Compare Hermit Crab's experience to the changes the students are experiencing as they are growing up. Do they ever feel that they just don't fit? How do they help themselves feel better? If they had to make a change, such as a move to a new grade level, a new school, or a new home, what types of things would they like to bring along with them to make the move easier? Have the students draw a picture of themselves in their changing situation and all the items or people they would like to bring with them.

5. Ask the children to decorate folders, which you will laminate, to hold all their research materials and/or observation journal pages on the tide pools and coral reefs.

6. Begin by having the children brainstorm in groups and as a class what things they specifically want to find out about the ocean. Using the Charting New Knowledge handout on page 57, the children can identify those specific areas they want to find out about beyond what you are teaching. This gives you an opportunity to show students the resources available so they can "take charge" of their learning.

7. Have the children work in pairs to do research on other animals in the Tide Pools.

8. Sing a variety of ocean-related songs. (See Bibliography, page 80.)

9. Do the Float an Egg Experiment (page 53). Why do things float better in salt water? How does this help the animals in the ocean?

10. Have the children read *Ralph's Narrow Escape*, pages 17-18. As a follow-up, have students write about a time they felt scared and how they handled it, and have them describe their special talents.

Overview of Activities *(cont.)*

EXTENDING THE BOOK

1. Have children bring in their own shell collections to study and classify, using *Audubon's Field Guide*. Displays can be made with shoeboxes, construction paper, and paper strips for labelling.

2. Write a class story titled "The Further Adventures of Hermit Crab." Map out a main problem, characters, and solution before beginning. Write the story on construction paper and have pairs of children illustrate each page. Laminate and bind into a class Big Book.

3. Create a bulletin board. Use a combination of children's work and real ocean artifacts to create this lively and interactive bulletin board. First, cover the bulletin board with blue paper. Then taking pieces of brown butcher paper, tear the paper in strips and layer them to show the rocky tide pool area. Pin on artifacts such as sea stars, barnacles, and coral to add some realism to your teaching board. Shells along the border are also a nice touch. Now, as the children begin creating the projects in this book, add the new artwork to your board—a board that, by the end of your study, illustrates the abundance of life found in the tide pools.

4. Ask your local high school if they have any sea creatures to share with your class. These may be preserved in formaldehyde, so you need to be careful about student handling, but they make an excellent display in your room.

5. Many pet stores will conduct tours of their facilities during and after school hours. Some of these have excellent salt water aquariums on site with their own thriving ocean ecosystems.

Things to Look for in a Tide Pool

These are some of the creatures you can find in a tide pool. Take this list to a tide pool or pet shop and see how many of them you can find hidden in the nooks and crannies of the rocky tide pools. Check them off as you find them and write down anything interesting you observe about the animals.

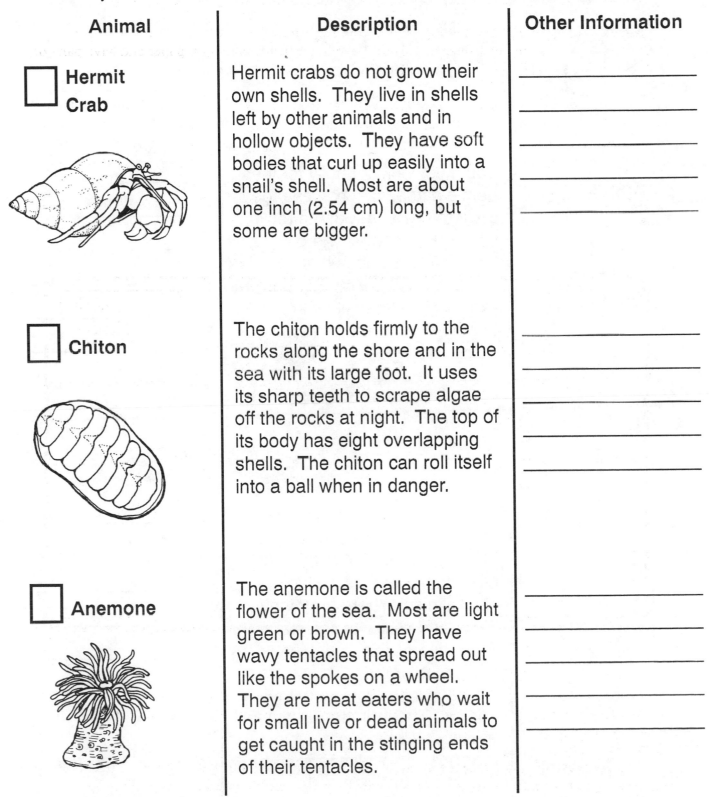

Animal	Description	Other Information
☐ Hermit Crab	Hermit crabs do not grow their own shells. They live in shells left by other animals and in hollow objects. They have soft bodies that curl up easily into a snail's shell. Most are about one inch (2.54 cm) long, but some are bigger.	_____ _____ _____ _____ _____
☐ Chiton	The chiton holds firmly to the rocks along the shore and in the sea with its large foot. It uses its sharp teeth to scrape algae off the rocks at night. The top of its body has eight overlapping shells. The chiton can roll itself into a ball when in danger.	_____ _____ _____ _____
☐ Anemone	The anemone is called the flower of the sea. Most are light green or brown. They have wavy tentacles that spread out like the spokes on a wheel. They are meat eaters who wait for small live or dead animals to get caught in the stinging ends of their tentacles.	_____ _____ _____ _____

Things to Look for in a Tide Pool *(cont.)*

Animal	Description	Other Information

Animal

☐ **Sea Snail**

☐ **Octopus**

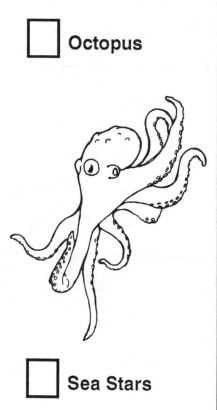

☐ **Sea Stars**

Description

These sea snails are found mainly under rocks. They are about one inch (2.54 cm) long. They have bluish-white shells with a felt-like covering of dark brown.

You must look carefully for the gentle octopus. It can change color to blend in with the rocks, seaweed, or coral where it hides. The octopus has no shell. It has very strong, parrot-like jaws and has eight arms that have suckers on them. Most octopuses are only as large as a person's fist, but some grow as large as 28 feet (8.4m) from the tip of one arm to another.

Most sea stars or starfish have five arms, which are called rays. They are attached to the central part of their bodies, called the central disc. There are many kinds and colors of sea stars. Some are purple, red, blue, orange, or yellow. They have a stomach in the middle of their bodies. They turn inside out to eat food. Starfish eat oysters, mussels, snails, limpets, crabs, barnacles, and sea urchins.

Other Information

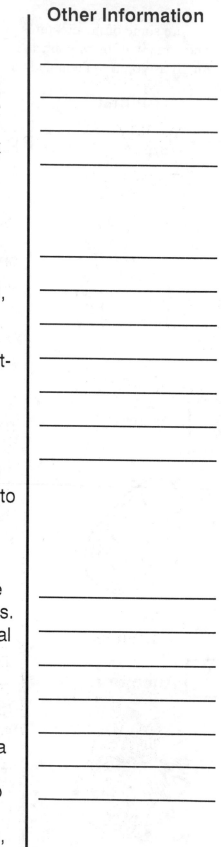

Things to Look for in a Tide Pool *(cont.)*

Animal	Description	Other Information

Animal   **Description**   **Other Information**

☐ **Sea Urchin**

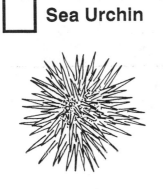

The sea urchin is in the same family of animals as the sea star. It has long, hard stinging spines that reach out from its body. The spines are from 1 to 10 inches (2.5 - 25 cm) across and can be purple, red, green, or orange.

_____

☐ **Barnacle**

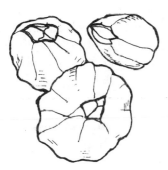

These shelled animals live upside down in their shells. They wave their feathery feet in the water. These feet trap plankton, the barnacles' food. Barnacles are found stuck on rocks and other large objects and live in large groups. Most barnacles are from ½ to 1 inch (1.3 - 2.5 cm) across.

_____

☐ **Goose Barnacle**

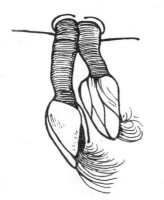

Goose barnacles have long necks called stalks. They are covered with many overlapping shells and stick firmly onto the rocks of the tide pools. The goose barnacles grow from one to six inches (2.5 - 15.2 cm) long, and they live in large groups.

_____

I'm a Crustacean

Hi! My name is Courtney, and I am a crab. I live in the ocean. I belong to a group of animals called crustaceans. All crustaceans have shells. That means our skeletons are on the outside of our bodies. We breathe through gills, just like fish. We have many pairs of legs, and our bodies are jointed, kind of like your elbows and knees. We use our feelers for touching, feeling, or smelling.

I have many crustacean cousins like the shrimp, lobster, and barnacle. Some crustaceans can swim, like the shrimp. Some of us can only scuttle along the ocean floor, like the lobster and me, the crab. The barnacle is a crustacean that sticks to a hard spot and never ever moves. I would not like that. Would you?

The hermit crab is also a crustacean, but he does not grow his own shell. He has to find empty shells of other animals to move into when he gets too big for his shell.

We all live in or around the water. I live in a tide pool, but some of my family live in the coral reefs, the deep ocean, and even in lakes. Come visit us sometime, will you?

1. All crustaceans have _____

2. How do crustaceans breathe? _____

   _____

3. Name three kinds of crustaceans. _____

   _____

Pretend you are a hermit crab looking for a home. On the back of this paper, write about how you would go about finding your new home.

Readers' Theater

Readers' Theater is a style of performance done by players standing before an audience. The players use only their voices to create characters and action. In order to perform Readers' Theater, students should understand its unique vocabulary. Review the list below with your students. Use these words when giving rehearsal directions.

Vocabulary

Script:	play or story to be read
Rehearsal:	practicing the play
Cast:	people in the play
Player:	person who is in the play
Understudy:	a player who learns the part of another player in case he/she is needed to substitute
Upstage:	toward the rear of the stage
Downstage:	toward the front of the stage
Performance:	the actual presentation of the play
Dress Rehearsal:	play rehearsal in costume (costumes are optional); last rehearsal before the performance
Bow:	bending at the waist to the audience for their applause
Audience:	people who watch the play
Offstage:	any area that is not the stage
Applause/Clapping:	gesture of gratitude from the audience

Rehearsal

Copy the Readers' Theater script (pages 14-16). Rehearse it several times to give hesitant readers self-confidence. Practice the script with the class using the following suggestions:

- *Model reading*—only the teacher reads
- *Echo reading*—teacher reads a line and students repeat it
- *Choral reading*—teacher and class read together
- Divide the class into groups of ten. Give each person a different part to read.
- Divide the class into ten groups. Give each group a part to read using choral speaking. Select one student who reads well to anchor the group.

Performance

Have ten students or ten groups perform Readers' Theater in front of the class. Students may wish to dress in black clothing so the words are emphasized. Ask the class to give compliments and offer constructive ideas for improvement. Then perform the play for another class. Readers' Theater is also an excellent idea for Parent Night or other school functions.

Hermit Crab Readers' Theater

Cast:

Narrators 1, 2, 3, 4	Lanternfish
Starfish	Sea Anemone
Sea Urchin	Sea Snail
Hermit Crab	Pebbles
Crusty Coral	Little Crab

Hermit Crab: Time to move. I've grown too big for this shell.

Narrator 1: Hermit Crab had felt safe and snug in his shell. But now it was too snug. He stepped out of the shell and onto the floor of the ocean, but it was frightening out in the open sea without a shell to hide in.

Hermit Crab: What if a big fish comes along and attacks me? I must find a new house soon.

Narrator 2: Early in February, Hermit Crab found just the house he was looking for. It was a big shell, and strong. He moved right in, wiggling and wiggling about inside it to see how it felt. It felt just right.

Hermit Crab: But it looks so—well, so plain.

Narrator 3: In March, Hermit Crab met some sea anemones. They swayed gently back and forth in the water.

Hermit Crab: How beautiful you are! Would one of you be willing to come and live on my house? It is so plain, it needs you.

Sea Anemone: I'll come.

Narrator 4: Gently, Hermit Crab picked up the sea anemone with his claw and put it on his shell. In April, Hermit Crab passed a flock of starfish moving slowly along the sea floor.

Hermit Crab: How handsome you are! Would one of you be willing to decorate my house?

Starfish: I would.

Narrator 1: Carefully, Hermit Crab picked up the starfish with his claw and put it on his house. In May, Hermit Crab discovered some coral. They were hard and didn't move.

Hermit Crab Readers' Theater (cont.)

Hermit Crab: How pretty you are! Would one of you be willing to help make my house more beautiful?

Crusty Coral: I would.

Narrator 2: Gingerly, Hermit Crab picked up the coral with his claw and placed it on his shell. In June, Hermit Crab came to a group of snails crawling over a rock on the ocean floor. They grazed as they went, picking up algae and bits of debris, and leaving a neat path behind them.

Hermit Crab: How tidy and hard-working you are! Would one of you be willing to come and help clean my house?

Sea Snail: I would.

Narrator 3: Happily, Hermit Crab picked up the snail with his claw and placed it on his shell. In July, Hermit Crab came upon several sea urchins. They had sharp, prickly needles.

Hermit Crab: How fierce you look! Would one of you be willing to protect my house?

Sea Urchin: I would.

Narrator 4: Gratefully, Hermit Crab picked up the sea urchin with his claw and placed it near his shell. In August, Hermit Crab and his friends wandered into a forest of seaweed.

Hermit Crab: It's so dark in here.

Sea Anemone: How dim it is!

Starfish: How gloomy it is!

Crusty Coral: How murky it is!

Sea Snail: I can't see!

Sea Urchin: It's like nighttime!

Narrator 1: In September, Hermit Crab spotted a school of lanternfish darting through the dark water.

Hermit Crab Readers' Theater *(cont.)*

Hermit Crab: How bright you are! Would one of you be willing to light up our house?

Lanternfish: I would!

Narrator 2: And the lanternfish swam over near the shell. In October, Hermit Crab approached a pile of smooth pebbles.

Hermit Crab: How smooth you are! Would you mind if I rearranged you?

Pebbles: Not at all.

Narrator 3: Hermit Crab picked the pebbles up one by one with his claw and built a wall around his shell.

Hermit Crab: Now my house is perfect!

Narrator 4: But in November, Hermit Crab felt that his shell seemed a bit too small. Little by little, over the year, Hermit Crab had grown. Soon he would have to find another, bigger home. But he had come to love his friends—the sea anemone, the starfish, the coral, the sea urchin, the snail, the lanternfish, and even the smooth pebbles.

Hermit Crab: My friends have been so good to me. They are like a family. How can I ever leave them?

Narrator 1: In December, a smaller hermit crab passed by.

Little Crab: I have outgrown my shell. Would you know of a place for me?

Hermit Crab: I have outgrown my house, too. I must move on. You are welcome to live here, but you must promise to be good to my friends.

Little Crab: I promise.

Narrator 2: The following January, Hermit Crab stepped out and the little crab moved in. He waved goodbye.

Hermit Crab: I couldn't stay in that little shell forever.

Narrator 3: The ocean floor looked wider than he had remembered, but Hermit Crab wasn't afraid. Soon he spied the perfect house—a big, empty shell. It looked, well, a little plain, but...

Hermit Crab: Sponges! Barnacles! Clown fish! Sand dollars! Electric eels! Oh, there are so many possibilities! I can't wait to get started!

Ralph's Narrow Escape

Read the story and color the pictures.

Ralph is an octopus. He lives in the tide pools. Ralph has a very special talent.
He can hide almost anywhere because he can change color. Every once in a
while, something big will come along and scare Ralph. His fear sends messages
to a part of his body that sends messages back to the rest of his body to change
color, almost any color in the rainbow. Ralph also has a special hose in his body
that squirts water out so quickly that Ralph can make a quick getaway. That hose
is called a *siphon*. Nobody can catch Ralph.

One day an orange Ralph was lying among the sponges when a shadow fell
across the tide pool. Ralph's three hearts started to pump wildly, but Ralph didn't
move. Ralph tilted his head to see a hand coming through the water. It picked up
his friend on the tide pool floor—Mr. Hermit Crab. Mr. Hermit Crab backed quickly
into his shell as soon as the hand touched him, but it was no use. Ralph heard
voices above laughing and squealing with delight as Mr. Hermit Crab tried to
scramble away.

17

Ralph's Narrow Escape *(cont.)*

Soon, the shadow fell across the tide pool again. This time Ralph could see the wavy figures of people as they peered into the pool. He felt very scared because he knew they were looking at him. One of the figures leaned into the tide pool with—oh, no—a net! Ralph's three hearts were beating faster than ever now. Quickly he sucked in as much water as he could and whoosh! He pushed it out of his siphon and darted backwards into a kelp bed.

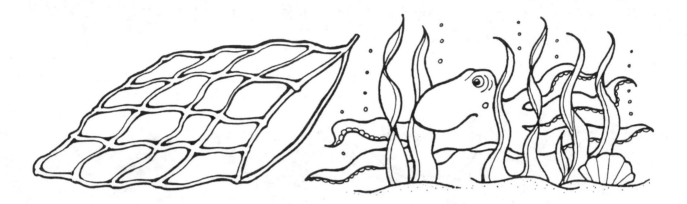

Ralph looked down and saw he was now a brownish gold. Whew! That was close. Ralph waited until the shadows passed away to peer out again. Nearby, a bed of mussels were rooted to a rock. After so much excitement, Ralph was ready for a good supper. He wrapped his legs around their shells and pulled and pulled and pulled until his arms ached. Finally the shells popped open, and Ralph ate his fill. A juicy snail passed by and Ralph curled an arm around it. The snail stuck to his suckers and made a nice dessert for Ralph.

The tide was coming in. Good! No more humans for a while. Ralph decided it was bedtime. This had been a scary day for the little octopus. So he moved to a hollow spot between two rocks and looked down to see his body change color. He was speckled brown now. He sighed and went to sleep.

Goodnight, Ralph!

Response Poetry

Response poetry is a form of free verse that uses a line-by-line suggestion method to draw poetic imagery from students. The teacher reads each line from a piece of poetry, allowing time for the students to write down their responses. At the end of the exercise, each child has an original poem.

Poetry Selection: "By the Sea" by Charlotte Zolotow and "Sea Shell" by Amy Lowell, (See Bibliography, page 80.) or other related poem.

Teacher Preparation: Write the poem "By the Sea" on sentence strips. Use one sentence strip for each line. Tape these to the chalkboard, leaving enough room under each line for a new line.

Setting the Stage: On another section of the board, brainstorm with the class all the words they can think of to describe the ocean. Cover as many sounds, sights, feelings, and smells as they can imagine. Encourage students to use active, descriptive words (e.g. waves crashing, thundering, etc.).

Procedure:

1. Tell the students that today they will create a poem, one that does not rhyme but creates pictures with words.

   As I read a line from a poem, you will tell me words that describe the pictures that come into your mind.

2. With the first sentence strip in place, read the first line and ask for a response from the class. Write that response on the line provided. Tape the second line up and repeat the process line by line. At the end, remove the Zolotow poem and reveal the student-generated poem below. Ask the students to title their work.

1st line of poem

blank for student response

2nd line of poem

blank for student response

3rd line of poem

blank for student response

3. Repeat the process on an individual basis. Each child writes his/her own reactions to each line.

4. Now that they have experience, try this process with a more complex poem such as Amy Lowell's "Sea Shell."

5. Art Extension: Rewrite the student poems on index cards and hang them from stuffed sea shells or sea stars.

Parallel Poetry

Read the poem "Until I Saw the Sea" by Lillian Moore. (See Bibliography, page 80.) Using the Charting New Knowledge handout (page 57), talk about many of the things the students have learned that they did not know about before beginning this study. Have the students generate their own "Until I Saw the Sea (Tide Pools, Coral Reefs)" poem, using the pattern below.

Example

"Until I Saw the Coral Reefs"

Until I saw the coral reefs

I did not know

That parrot fish were blue and pink

Or clown fish were orange

I never knew

That coral grew in so many shapes,

Sizes, and amazing colors

Nor did I know before

That underneath the ocean

Was a beautiful, silent world

Waiting to be seen.

Until I Saw the _____

Until I saw the _____

I did not know

_____

_____

_____

I never knew

_____

_____

_____

Nor did I know before

_____

_____

_____

Marine Math

Draw pictures in the space provided to show these math problems. Then color and count them and write your answer.

1. Six clown fish are swimming in the coral reef. Each clown fish has two white stripes. How many white stripes do you see?

_____

white stripes

2. Each starfish has five arms it uses to crawl along the rocky shore. Five starfish are searching for clams. How many arms can you find?

_____

arms

3. Three octopuses are hiding among the rocks. Every one of the "octos" has eight arms. How many octopus arms are there?

_____

octopus arms

4. The inky squids each have ten tentacles. Two squids float past you while you swim. How many tentacles float past?

_____

tentacles

5. The crab has two bulging eyes to see its prey. Four crabs scuttle sideways along the colored reef. How many eyes are looking about?

_____

eyes

Hatch Brine Shrimp Eggs

It is difficult to keep most sea animals in an aquarium because they need plenty of oxygen which they usually get when the waves stir up the water. However, the brine shrimp are easy to keep whether you live near the sea or inland.

The eggs of this tiny crustacean are collected from the edges of salt lakes in the United States and sold in pet shops. The eggs will last for years if kept dry and stored in a fairly cool place.

Step One:

Boil about 1 cup (.25 L) of tap water and leave to cool.

Step Two:

Tip some of the eggs into a wide-necked glass jar. Add half a tablespoon (7.5 mL) of cooking salt. Do not use iodized salt.

Step Three:

Add the cooled tap water and stir. Mark the level of the water on the outside with a piece of tape. Leave the jar in a warm place. If the water level begins to fall, add more tap water that has been boiled and cooled. There is no need to add salt since it does not evaporate with the water.

Step Four:

After 40 hours, watch for the eggs to hatch. Use a magnifier to see them.

The brine shrimp feed on bacteria. Bacteria will grow in the water if you put in a tiny piece of lettuce or cabbage. The piece of leaf should not be any bigger than your fingernail. Put a new piece in the water when the last piece is gone.

Every few days pour the shrimp and salt water into a new clean jar since more oxygen dissolves in the water as you pour it.

At Home in the Coral Reef

by Katy Muzik

This book allows its readers to follow the development of the coral polyp from its release as an egg through the planula's, or baby coral's, search for a home. Through colorful illustrations and informative and imaginative text, At Home in the Coral Reef *describes the underwater communities, plant life, and fascinating animals the planula meets on its journey to its new habitat. Some of the animals shown are the butterfly fish, the barracuda, the brittle star, the grouper, and the shrimp. Also mentioned are some man-made problems which threaten the coral reefs.*

Sample Plan

Day 1
- Make a Coral Reef Mini Book. (pages 29-31)
- Introduce words from the Word Bank. (page 26)
- Read *At Home in the Coral Reef.*
- Learn about scuba equipment. (page 32)

Day 2
- How Do You Feed a Coral Polyp? (page 33)
- Do Water Creature Feature experiment. (page 34)
- Read other books about tide pools and coral reefs. Do the accompanying activities. (page 28)
- Begin making salt dough coral reef. (page 37)

Day 3
- Play the Race to the Reef game. (pages 41-43)
- Make fresh water from salt water. (page 53)
- Complete Aquarium Math. (page 44)

- Reread Coral Reef Mini-Book.
- Find out if water has weight. (page 54)

Day 4
- Continue working on the salt dough coral reef.
- Create a Coral Life Cycle Viewer. (pages 38-39)
- Find out the color of sea water. (page 40)
- Try sandy measurement. (pages 47-48)
- Sing a song about the coral reef. (page 73)
- Clean an oil spill. (page 51)

Day 5
- Prepare some Simple Sea Recipes. (page 75)
- Play Race to the Reef game. (pages 41-43)
- Finish salt dough coral reef.
- Learn the ways to help the environment. (page 52)
- Reread *At Home in the Coral Reef.*
- Plan culminating activity. (page 76)

Overview of Activities

SETTING THE STAGE

1. If possible, show students a piece of coral. Let them touch it and feel how hard and rough it is. Write "plant", "animal", and "rock" on the board. Ask students to tell you in which group coral belongs. Most will probably say rock. Surprise them by telling them that coral is an animal and what they have been feeling are the skeletons of many of those animals.

   Ask them where their own skeletons are located (inside their bodies). Our bodies use calcium to keep our bones strong and growing. Coral polyps (coral animals) make their skeletons by taking calcium out of the sea water and depositing it as calcium carbonate (limestone) around the outside of the lower half of their bodies. Most polyps are less than one inch (2.5 cm) across; however, so many polyps live so closely to each other that their skeletons stick together to form large formations called reefs. For example, The Great Barrier Reef, the largest in the world, is a broken chain of coral reefs along the northeast coast of Australia that extends for about 1,250 miles (2,010 km).

2. Have students make a Coral Reef Mini-Book. Direct them to color the pictures and staple the pages together. Read and discuss the mini book.

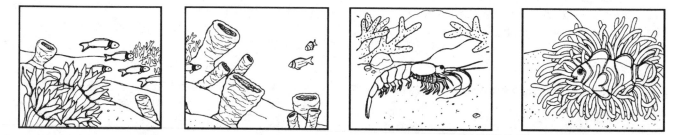

3. Introduce the book by showing the cover and telling about the author and illustrator. Katy Muzik, the author of *At Home in the Coral Reef*, is a marine biologist who has dived among coral reefs all over the world. She wrote the book to help children appreciate this fragile sea environment so that they will see the need to help preserve and protect the coral reefs. It is illustrated by Katherine Brown-Wing, who works as a biological illustrator for both scientific journals and children's books.

ENJOYING THE BOOK

1. Read and discuss the book *At Home in the Coral Reef.* Take time with the book so students can have fun searching the big picture to locate and name the species shown in the individual pictures. Be sure to emphasize the words in the word bank.

2. Direct students to complete the coral reef vocabulary activity by filling in the blanks to complete the sentences about coral reefs.

3. Use page 32 to learn about divers and the equipment they use when they go underwater to study coral reefs. Discuss the importance the careful scuba diver places on not harming the coral by touching it or taking it away from the reef. Also discuss the fact that much more was known about land plants and animals than underwater plants and animals before scientists had the equipment to study life underwater.

4. Name That Coral, page 35, will help students identify different types of coral.

Overview of Activities *(cont.)*

ENJOYING THE BOOK *(cont.)*

5. Students will gain a better understanding that coral is an animal by making the Coral Life Cycle Viewer on pages 38-39.

6. Explain that coral, because it is an animal, needs to eat. Do the How Do You Feed a Coral Polyp? handout on page 33.

7. How are animals of the tide pools and coral reefs different from other creatures of the ocean? For one thing, they have less water pressure bearing down on them. Do the Does Water Have Weight? experiment on page 54.

8. Aquarium Math, on page 44, will allow students to practice their addition skills as they calculate how much a complete aquarium would cost.

9. Use the Water Creature Feature experiment on page 34 to view plankton closely. Students will have fun looking for the strange tiny plants and creatures under the microscope.

10. Sing the song "Down by the Sea" on page 73. Encourage students to think of their own verses based on animals that live in the coral reefs.

EXTENDING THE BOOK

1. Have students make salt dough coral reefs as described on page 37. Encourage them to think of ways to represent different kinds of coral.

2. The Race to the Reef game (pages 41-43) will give students information about coral reefs and some things that could harm them.

3. You Can Help!, page 52, will give students ideas for ways to protect the environment. Have students add their own ideas to the list.

4. The Tide Pool/Coral Reef research center will allow students to find more information about animals that live in the tide pools and coral reefs.

5. Write or call the Cousteau Society for information on membership and a subscription to their excellent children's magazine, *Dolphin Log*. The cost is minimal and the magazine is filled with interesting articles and beautiful underwater photography geared to a child's level of understanding.

The Cousteau Society Membership Center

870 Greenbrier Circle, Suite 402

Chesapeake, VA 23320 (804) 523-9335

Word Bank

At Home in the Coral Reef contains some words with which students may not be familiar. When reading the book, be sure to point out the following words in context and have the students try to determine their meanings.

coral reef

tentacles

planula

lagoon

current

crest

bacteria

coral polyp

zillion

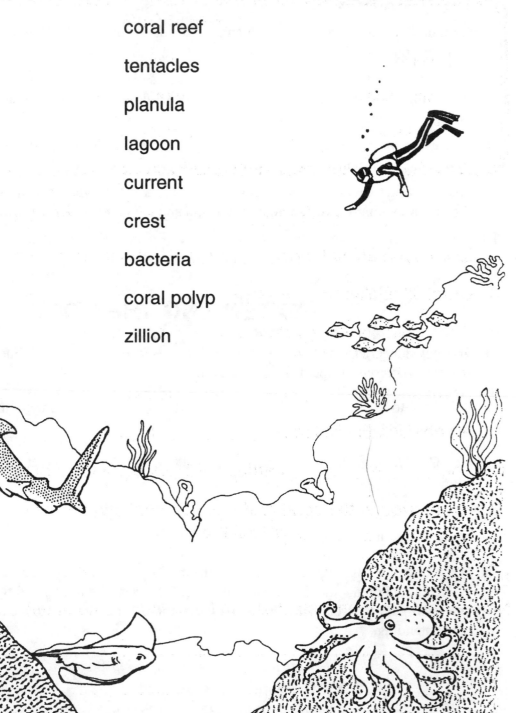

Coral Reef Vocabulary Activity

Find out some facts about the coral reefs and the animals that live there. Fill in the blanks with words from the word bank.

Word Bank

polyp	bacteria	skeletons
coral reefs	current	eggs
tentacles	planula	

---

1. __ __ r __ __ __ ee __ __ are built slowly by zillions of coral animals.

2. Each coral animal, or p __ __ y __, is about the size of a pencil eraser.

3. Coral, like jellyfish, use their __ __ __ t __ __ __ __ s to capture their food.

4. Coral animals live so closely together that their __ k __ __ __ t__ __ __ are connected.

5. Coral releases its __ g __ __ once a year.

6. A baby coral is called a __ l __ __ __ l __.

7. The __ __ rr __ __ __ carries the baby coral to its new home.

8. Water around the coral reef must be kept clean or harmful b__ __ __ __ __ __ a will kill the coral.

Bonus

Name three other animals that can be found in a coral reef.

1. _____

2. _____

3. _____

What Lives Here?

These informative and visually stimulating books will help teachers and children answer many questions about life in tide pools and coral reefs.

At Home in the Tide Pool by Alexandra Wright (1992, Charlesbridge Publishing, 85 Main Street, Watertown, MA 02172, Phone 617-926-0329. Available in Canada from Monarch Books, in the UK from Cazelle Book Services and in Australia from Encyclopedia Britannica.)

This book follows the same format as *At Home in the Coral Reef*, and answers the question, "What is a tide pool?" beautifully. Students will enjoy reading this book written by twelve-year-old Alexandra Wright, which she wrote after spending a summer at science camp where tide pools were explored. The illustrations by Marshall Peck III provide an accurate look at the amazing diversity of nature found in a tide pool.

Coral Reef by Barbara Taylor (1992, A Dorling Kindersley Book, Houghton Mifflin Publishers, Wayside Road, Burlington, Massachusetts 01803, Phone 800-225-3362)

The close-up photography by Jane Burton provides children with a clear view of the many wondrous animals found in a coral reef. Symbiotic relationships are explored throughout the text so readers see that all animals serve a purpose in keeping the reef healthy. Each page has a Guess What? skin diver who provides additional information.

Using *Coral Reef* and *At Home in the Tide Pool*

1. Take a trip to a tide pool, or to an aquarium that simulates one, if at all possible, so children can get a first-hand look at the fascinating animals that call a tide pool home. In addition, you might bring in specimens from seafood shops, shell collections, or backyards (snails), so children can have a hands-on experience with tide pool, coral reef or similar creatures. Mussels are often available and children will enjoy using the diagram of the inside of a mussel in *At Home in the Tide Pool* to find the labeled parts on a real mussel.

2. To follow up the study of these books, have children choose one of the tide pool or coral reef animals and create a likeness of it. Any materials may be used, but many of these creatures lend themselves to food sculptures. For example: cucumber and parsley could become a sea cucumber; almonds layered with peanut butter could make a twelve-scaled worm; and a sea urchin could be created from an orange and toothpicks. Then set up your own tide pool or coral reef in the classroom using a tabletop or a child's wading pool, real rocks, and your students' models. Cover the pool or table with blue plastic wrap to simulate water.

3. Make an aquarium from two plastic two-liter bottles. Cut the top off one of the bottles. Next, you will need to steam the plastic base off the other bottle to fit over the cut end. Because of the small holes in the plastic base, the cover is ventilated. Ask the local pet store about donating rocks and small fish to complete your aquariums.

4. Contact a local dive shop about guest speakers. Most shops have certification classes which utilize a variety of slides and equipment to teach their programs and may be able to adapt a presentation which will enthrall young listeners.

CORAL REEF MINI BOOK

Name

Coral reefs are found in the warm parts of the oceans. They are giant "sea gardens" and are filled with brightly colored sea animals. Coral grows only where the water is warm.

The coral reefs are made from the skeletons of billions of tiny animals called coral polyps. They build up from the seabed to form weird and wonderful shapes.

The top part of the reef is living coral that colors the skeleton mountains with beautiful shades of orange, green, purple and yellow.

Brightly colored fish, like the clown fish and the parrot fish, swim in and out of the coral. Shellfish, such as crabs and clams, live among the many hiding places in the reef. Other sea creatures, such as sea anemones, sea urchins, sea fans, and sponges fasten onto the coral.

Coral Polyp

Soft living coral live on the top part of the reef. The coral polyp's tiny, feathery tentacles reach out of its shell at night to trap plankton. When the coral animal dies, it leaves a hard limestone skeleton. New coral polyps attach and grow on top of these skeletons.

Sponges

Sponges area animals that grow in many shapes and sizes. They live attached to rocks or plants for all their adult life. They feed on plankton found in the water that passes through their bodies.

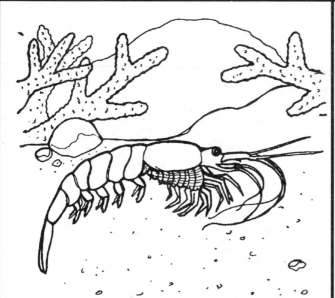

Shrimp

There are many different kinds of shrimp. Most shrimp are gray, brown, white, or pink, but some are bright red, blue, green or yellow. Shrimp have been called the trash collectors of the ocean world because they feed on dead or dying animal and plant life.

Clown Fish

The clown fish is a brightly colored red or orange fish with two white bands on its body. It swims safely among the stinging tentacles of the sea anemone. The clown fish is not hurt by the anemone's sting. The anemone's tentacles keep the clown fish safe from its enemies. In return, the anemone gets to share the clown fish's leftover food.

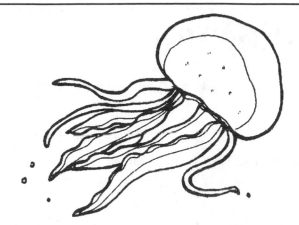

Jellyfish

Jellyfish float in the sea. They look like clear bells with thin streamers called tentacles hanging from them. Their bodies are mostly made of water. Most jellyfish tentacles hold bubbles, which shoot out threads of poison. These paralyze the victims. Some jellyfish are no bigger than a pinhead, and some have been known to have bodies eight feet (2.4m) long and tentacles measuring over two hundred feet (60m) long.

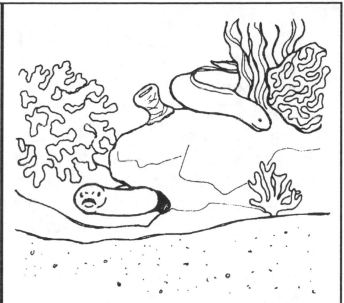

Moray Eels

Moray eels are scary-looking fish that look like prehistoric animals when they swim. They range in size from 60 cm to 2 m (2-6 feet) long. They hide in cracks and crevices among the coral and feed on smaller fish. They are harmless to people unless disturbed.

Sharks

There are over 250 kinds of sharks, and even though some kinds are dangerous to people, most are not. The shark is a fish, but it is different from other fish in many ways. They have no bones, only cartilage. Most fish lay eggs, but some sharks give birth to live young.

Parrot Fish

These blue and pink fish have mouths that look like a parrot's beak. Their bright colors blend in with the waters and coral of the reef. They use their strong teeth and parrot-shaped mouths to scrape away the shells of coral so they can feed on the living polyps underneath.

Be a Careful Diver

Careful scuba divers know never to touch the coral reef or they can harm the coral polyps that live there.

A scuba diver uses portable metal tanks of compressed air to breathe. One tank will allow a diver to stay 40 feet (12 meters) underwater for about an hour. The word "scuba" stands for self-contained underwater breathing apparatus. Divers wear face masks, wet suits, gloves, air tanks, and swim fins. They use snorkels while swimming at the surface of the water to conserve the air in their tanks.

To the right is a picture of a scuba diver. Use the following words to label the equipment.

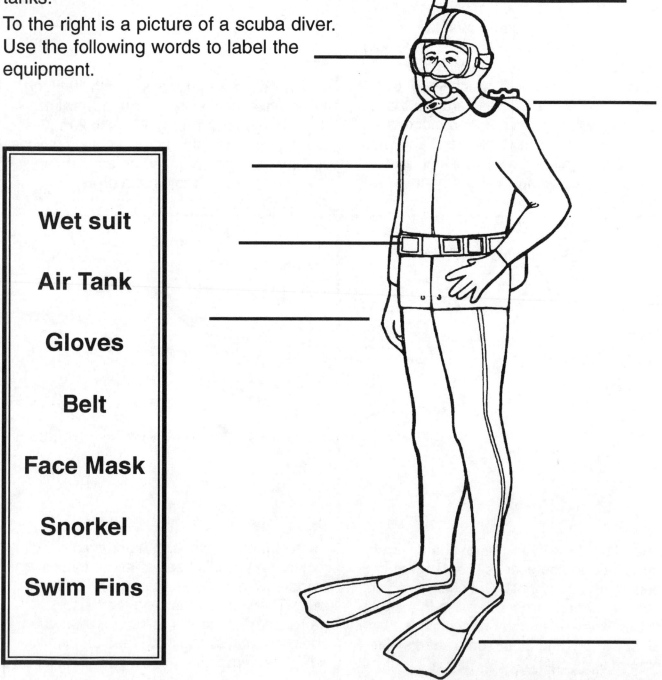

Wet suit

Air Tank

Gloves

Belt

Face Mask

Snorkel

Swim Fins

How Do You Feed a Coral Polyp?

Coral polyps get their food in two ways. One way is from the little green plants that grow inside each coral animal. These plants use the sun to make food. Some of this food is passed to the coral.

Another way polyps get their food is by trapping tiny underwater plants and animals with their tentacles. These plants and animals are called plankton, and you would need a microscope to see them clearly.

Color the microscopic views of the two ways plankton get their food.

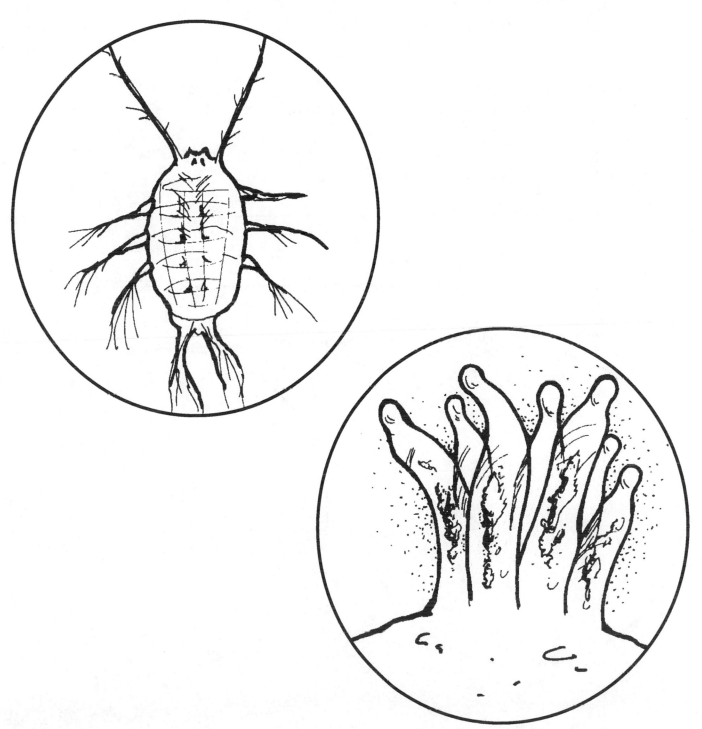

Water Creature Feature

We know that the plankton that feeds the coral reef are very tiny, but just how tiny? Try this simple observation and find out how small they actually are.

You will need the following:

- A microscope
- An eyedropper
- Microscope slides and covers
- Fresh sea, pond, or lake water

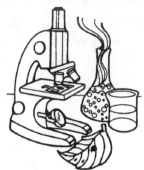

Procedure:

Working with a friend, place a small drop of the fresh sea, pond, or lake water onto the slide and cover it carefully. Clamp it under the lens and look through the viewfinder. Adjust the viewfinder until you see the strange shapes clearly.

Draw what you found under the microscope. These weird creatures might be a meal for a coral polyp.

Use at least three words to describe what you found.

1. _____

2. _____

3. _____

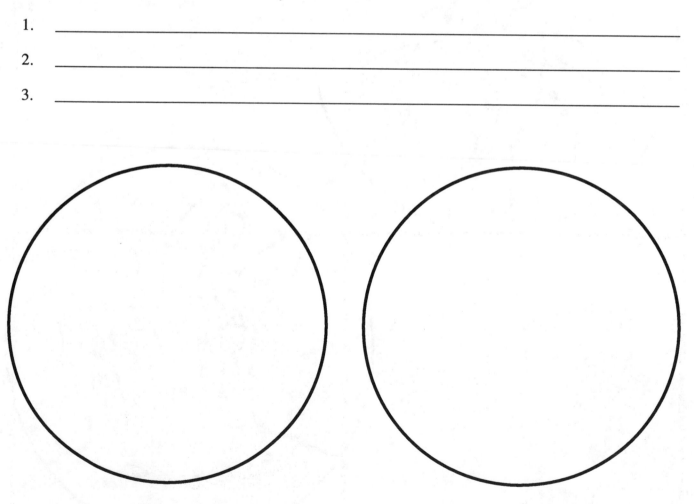

Name That Coral

There are many different kinds of coral. Different kinds of coral form different shapes. Read the descriptions of different kinds of coral, and then label the pictures with the correct names.

Staghorn coral looks like deer antlers.

Plate coral is big and flat, like a giant dinner plate.

Brain coral looks like a human brain because of its furrows and ridges.

Sea fans are soft coral with flexible skeletons. They can bend and sway like tree branches.

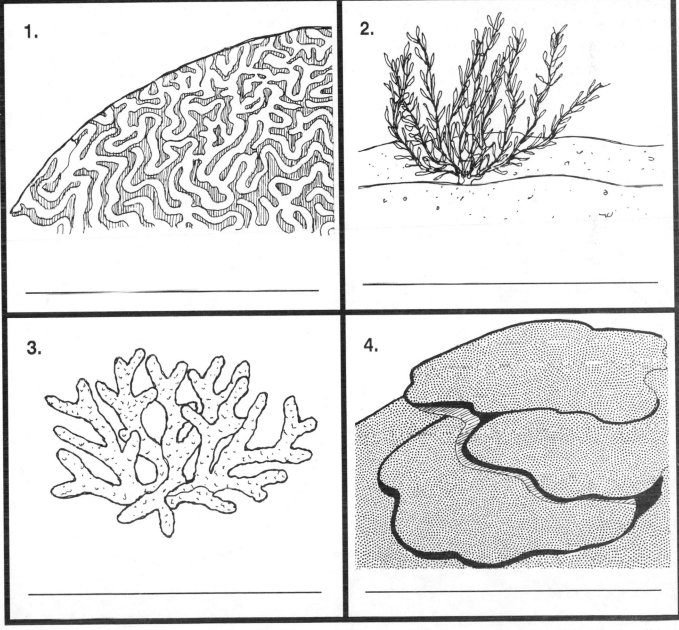

1. _____

2. _____

3. _____

4. _____

Coral Reef Directions

Look at the picture, then circle the best answer for each question.

1. What is directly above the parrot fish?

    A. Scuba diver

    B. Octopus

    C. Eel

2. What is to the left of the shark?

    A. Shrimp

    B. Octopus

    C. Parrot fish

3. What is directly to the right of the jellyfish?

    A. Eel

    B. Shark

    C. Octopus

4. What is directly to the left of the eel?

    A. Shrimp

    B. Scuba diver

    C. Parrot fish

5. What is below the scuba diver?

    A. Parrot fish

    B. Octopus

    C. Shark

Make a Salt Dough Coral Reef

Materials

- large mixing bowl
- paper bowls
- several colors of tempera paint
- small tree branch, or twig
- flour
- salt
- water

Directions

1. Make a large batch of salt dough. Mix 4 cups (.9 L) of flour with 1 cup (236 mL) of salt. Add 1 ½ cups (350 mL) warm water and knead until the mixture forms a pastry-like dough.

2. Have students turn their bowls upside-down and poke their branches or twigs through the bowls. They should then cover the twigs with the salt dough.

3. Let the twigs dry for approximately three or four days. Have the students paint their bowls and the twigs with tempera paint to resemble a coral reef.

Coral Life Cycle Viewer

Cut out the wheel below and color the pictures. Cut out and color the diver's mask on page 39. Cut along the dashed lines to make a window. Punch out the hole in the center on both the wheel and window. Punch out the hole in the center on both the wheel and mask. Using a paper fastener attach the wheel behind the mask. Rotate the wheel until the number one picture shows up in the window. Read the story by moving the wheel clockwise.

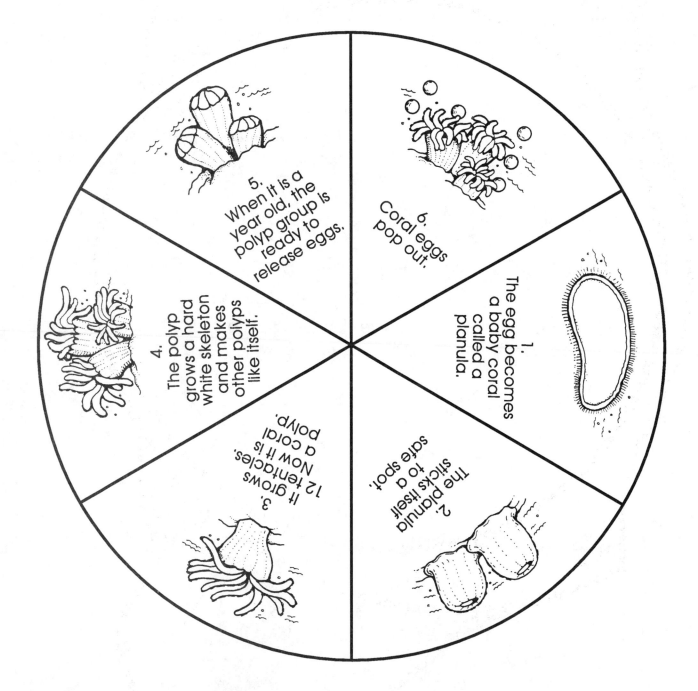

Coral Life Cycle Viewer

(cont.)

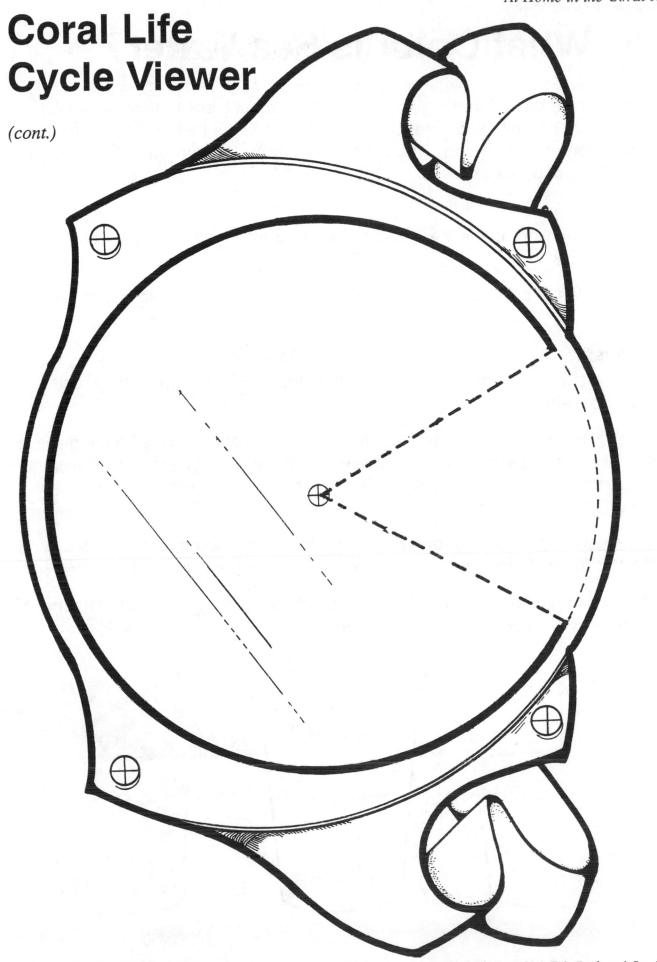

What Color Is Sea Water?

If you compared the color of a glass of tap water with a glass of sea water, you probably could not tell the difference. But, if you go to the beach, the ocean may look blue, gray, or dark green. The ocean water doesn't actually change color; it reflects the color of the sky.

Materials:

For every two children: one liter glass container or water glass filled with salt water.

Various shades of blue, black, and gray construction paper cut into 5" (13 cm) squares.

Directions:

1. Ask the students if they have ever been to the ocean or a lake. What color was the water?

2. Point to the salt water in the glass and ask what color the water in the glass is. Explain that if this water had been taken from the ocean it would be essentially the same color. So why do we think of the ocean in the various shades described?

3. Tell children to cover the top of the glass with dark blue construction paper. What happens? Why?

4. Have children use the various other colors to cover the glass. What happens? How does this explain the colors of the ocean?

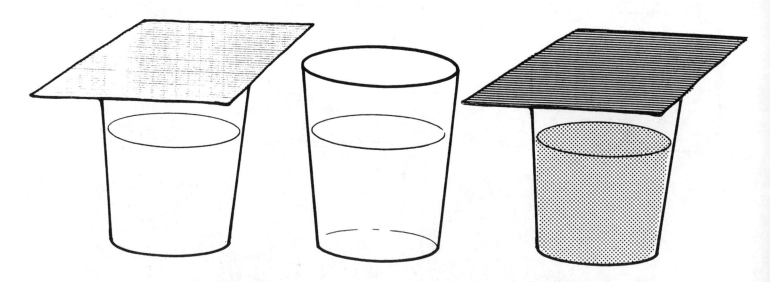

Race to the Reef

This is a game for two to four players.

Preparation:

Color the playing pieces. For more durability, the pieces may be taped to a coin. Color the gameboard and laminate, if desired.

The object of the game is to be the first player to reach the Coral Reef Finish.

How to Play:

Students place playing pieces on the spot marked "Island Start." Players roll die to move around the gameboard. A player must follow the directions on the space he or she lands on. If the space is blank, the player does nothing and waits for his or her next turn. If a space directs a student to move to the Coral Reef, the playing piece should be placed on the space marked "Coral Reef." Any time a player has to move back to the island, he or she should move to the space called "Island Start." Play continues until one player reaches the Coral Reef Finish.

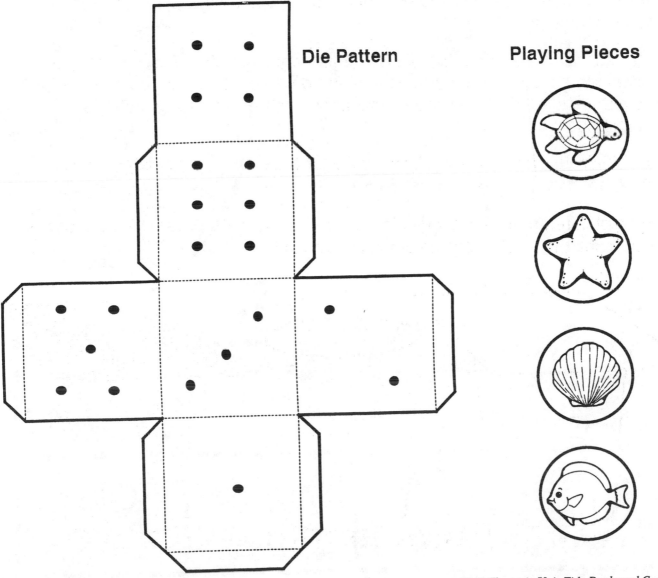

Die Pattern   **Playing Pieces**

Race to Coral Reef

Photograph a Barracuda. Move ahead three spaces.

Find a shark's tooth. Move ahead two spaces.

Get stung by a jellyfish. Move back five spaces.

Boat drops anchor on coral reef. Move back three spaces.

Washed ashore by waves. Move back four spaces.

Buy new scuba gear. Move to Coral Reef.

Oil Spill. Lose a turn.

See a hermit crab. Move ahead three spaces.

High Tide! Move back to Island Start.

CORAL REEF

Gameboard

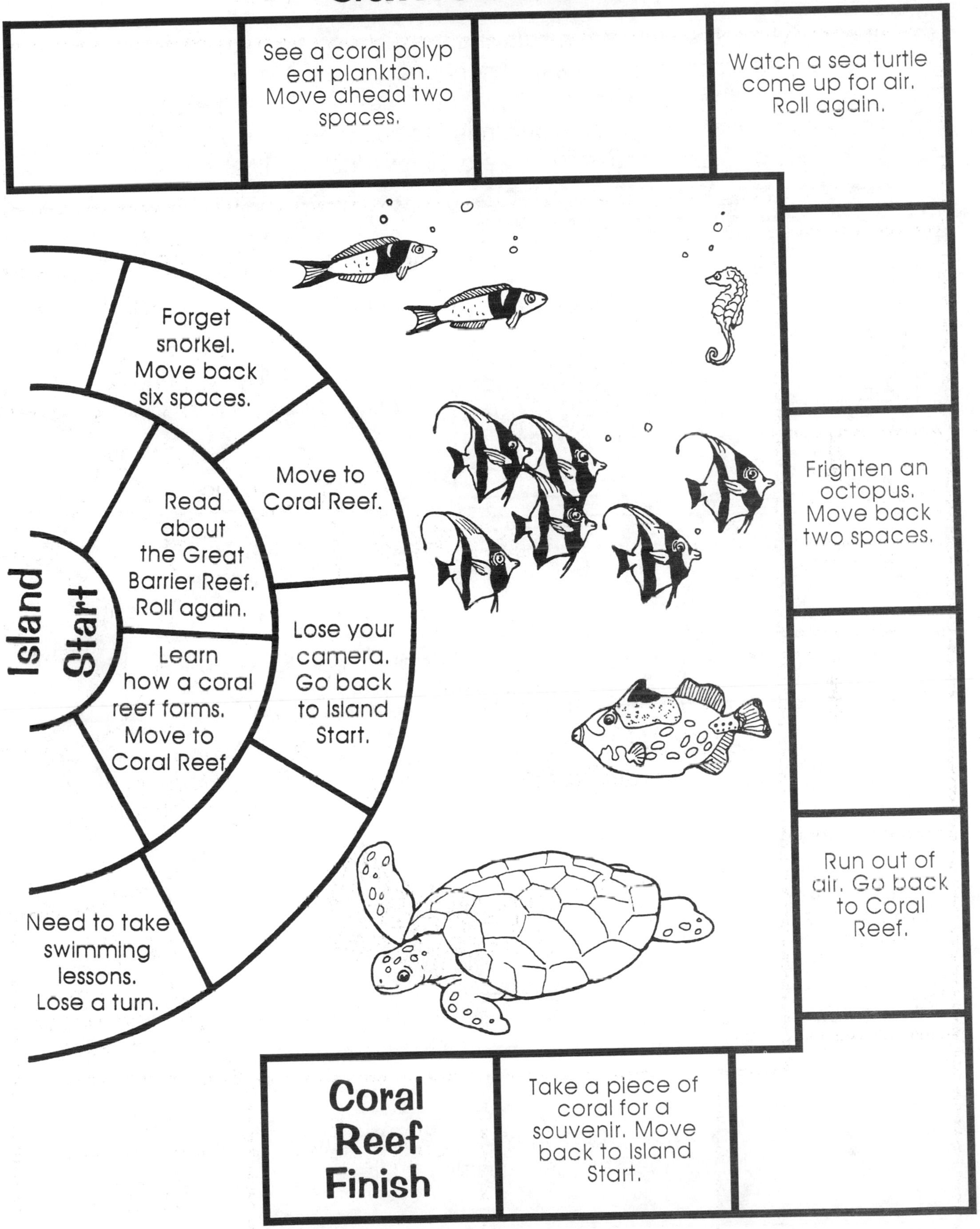

See a coral polyp eat plankton. Move ahead two spaces.

Watch a sea turtle come up for air. Roll again.

Forget snorkel. Move back six spaces.

Move to Coral Reef.

Read about the Great Barrier Reef. Roll again.

Island Start

Learn how a coral reef forms. Move to Coral Reef.

Lose your camera. Go back to Island Start.

Frighten an octopus. Move back two spaces.

Need to take swimming lessons. Lose a turn.

Run out of air. Go back to Coral Reef.

Coral Reef Finish

Take a piece of coral for a souvenir. Move back to Island Start.

Aquarium Math

Jessica and Kyle had so much fun studying the tide pools and coral reefs, they decided to put together their own salt water aquarium at home. That way they could see many of their favorite animals all the time. Mr. Price, the pet store owner, explained everything they would need to create their own tide pool ecosystem. Help Jessica and Kyle figure out how much it will all cost.

Price List

Sea anemone—$4.00	Sea snail—$2.00
Sea star—$7.00	Sea horse—$6.00
Sea fans—$8.00	Jellyfish—$3.00
Clown fish—$16.00	Barnacles—$1.00

Hermit Crab —$4.00

1. They bought a 20 gallon tank on sale for $42.00, a filter for $25.00, and rocks, sand, and gravel for $7.00. How much did they spend all together?

   _____

2. Jessica bought a sea anemone and a sea star. What did she pay for both animals?

   _____

3. Kyle bought 2 sea fans and 1 clown fish. How much did all three animals cost?

   _____

4. The children bought 4 sea snails and 2 hermit crabs. How much did they spend?

   _____

5. They decided to add 1 sea horse, 2 jellyfish, and 3 barnacles to their aquarium. What was the total cost of all 6 items?

   _____

6. What was the total amount of money that Jessica and Kyle spent on their aquarium? (You may need to use a calculator.)

   _____

44

Daily Writing Topics

1. Imagine you are marooned on a deserted island. Describe what it is like.

2. Describe the best vacation you have ever taken.

3. Imagine you are a tide pool animal. Write about your life.

4. If you could go on any vacation in the world, where would you go and why? What would you see there?

5. Tell what you would do and see if you were a scuba diver.

6. You are a drop of water in the ocean. Tell about your life from its beginning (life in the sea) to your trip to the clouds (as vapor) and back to the sea.

7. Write a story about how the sea urchin got his spines or how the clown fish got his stripes.

8. You are a scientist working at a tide pool lab on a secret formula. You drop some formula on yourself and the next thing you know, you are the size of a small shrimp and are swimming among the tide pool creatures. Describe your adventure.

9. Write an acrostic poem about an animal of the tide pools/coral reefs or about an island.

10. One day you come home to discover an octopus in your bathtub. He wants to go to school with you. Tell what happens.

11. Write a report about a tide pool/coral reef animal.

12. Describe a time you made a big change in your life, such as a move to a new home, a new school, or a new grade level. What feelings did you experience and how did you or other people make the move easier?

13. You are an animal of the ocean looking for a home. Describe your search.

14. You are an animal living in the coral reef. Which are you, predator or prey? Describe your search for food or how you hide from the predators.

15. Using all five senses (sight, taste, smell, hearing, touch), describe a trip to the seashore.

16. Write a six line picture book on "The Important Thing About the Ocean (Coral Reef/Tide Pool) Is...."

Ocean Haiku

Haiku is a Japanese form of non-rhyming poetry that employs a simple three-line format. The first line consists of 5 syllables, the second line has 7 syllables, and the third line has 5 syllables.

Syllables are like musical notes or beats. Each word has a certain number of beats to it. Use clapping to illustrate the beats or syllables in each child's name. Share the example.

Ocean

Salty, wet, wavy

Blue-green, aqua, and navy

Home to many fish

Brainstorm sensory words which describe the ocean. You may wish to play ocean sounds while this takes place. Have the class suggest some of these words to help form a class haiku about the ocean.

Now have each child make up his or her own haiku. After writing a haiku, have students copy it near the middle of a piece of paper. Have them cut the bottom of the paper to resemble waves, as shown in the illustration. Then have them fold the bottom of the paper over their poems.

Example:

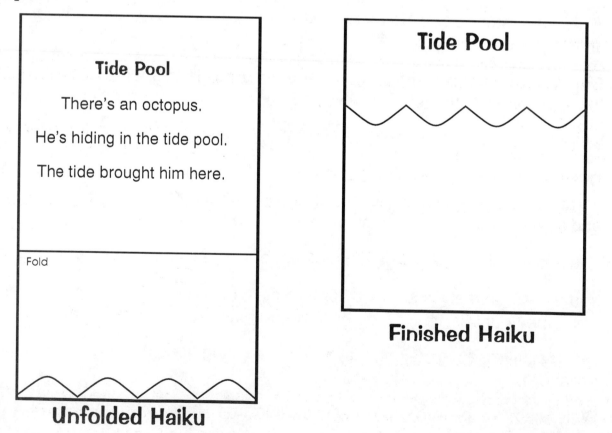

Tide Pool

There's an octopus.

He's hiding in the tide pool.

The tide brought him here.

Fold

Unfolded Haiku

Tide Pool

Finished Haiku

Sandy Measurement

Young children enjoy building sand castles and playing in the sand. They will also love working with sand in this activity where they explore the relationship between standard and non-standard units of measurement.

For this activity you will need:
- large trays
- sand
- scoops (coffee, detergent, etc.)
- 8 oz. (250 mL) cups or milk containers
- pint (500 mL) milk containers
- quart (1 L) milk containers
- gallon (4 L) milk containers
- permanent maker

Teacher Preparation
1. Cut the tops off the milk cartons so children can scoop and pour sand in and out of the containers easily. (You may wish to ask parents to send in containers.)

2. Mark each container according to its unit of measure.

3. Have students seated in groups of five to six children. Each group should have one large tray filled with sand and at least one of each of the following: scoop, cup, pint, quart, or gallon containers.

Procedure:
1. Give each group a time of exploration with the materials. After ten minutes or so, ask the students if they noticed anything about the various scoops and containers. Brainstorm and list these on the board.

2. Talk about standard units of measure. Have the children experiment and see if they can see any relationship between the measuring tools (e.g. if a certain amount of one measuring tool equals another). After a few minutes, list their responses.

3. Pass out the Sandy Mcasurement handout on page 48. Have groups work together to explore answers.

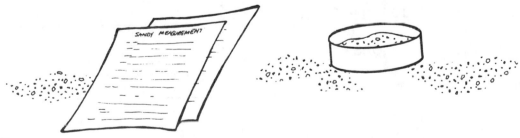

Extension:
Have students bring in various other scoops and measuring tools. Set up a tray or, better yet, a small, inflatable child's pool filled with sand as a center in the room. Children can explore relationships between standard and non-standard measurements on their own.

Sandy Measurement *(cont.)*

Work with your group to find the answers below.

A.   2 cups equal _____ pint.

B.   4 cups equal _____ quart.

C.   2 pints equal _____ .

D.   4 quarts equal _____ .

E.   8 cups equal _____ .

F.   6 cups equal_____ or _____ quart and ____ pint.

G.   1 quart equals _____ pints or _____ cups.

H.   1 gallon equals_____ pints or _____ quarts or _____ cups.

Bonus:

A. How many cups in 1 gallon + 1 quart + 1 pint? _____

B. How many pints in 3 gallons? _____

C. How many quarts in two gallons? _____

Graph Your Favorite Tide Pool Animal

Materials: 3" x 3" (8 cm x 8 cm) blank pieces of paper; graphing or butcher paper chart with headings for 5-6 tide pool animals (starfish, hermit crab, octopus, sea anemone, sea urchin, etc.). Have children color a picture of their favorite tide pool animals from the pictures below and glue them to a chart.

Sample Questions and Graph:

1. Which animal was the favorite?
2. Which animal did the fewest people choose?
3. How many more people chose __octopus__ than chose __sea star__?
4. How many children chose __hermit crab__ and __sea urchin__ all together?

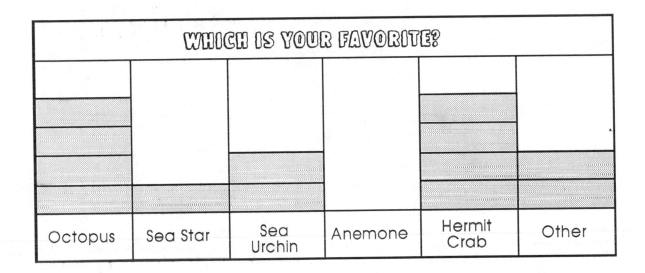

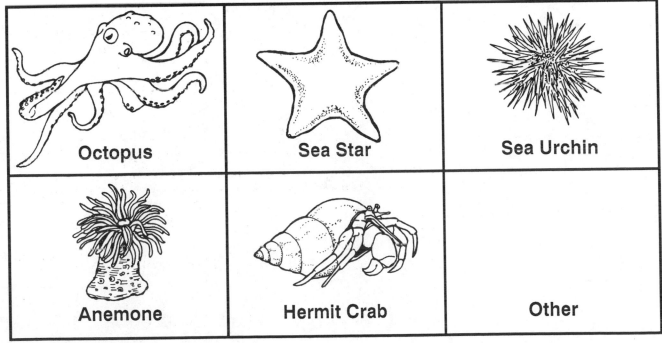

Crab Walk

Crabs are excellent scavengers. They pick up animal and plant leftovers as they travel through the ocean. Most crabs move sideways across the rocks, coral, and sandy bottom of the sea floor. Use your ruler to measure in centimeters the distance each crab crawls as it "cleans up" on his trip through his ocean home.

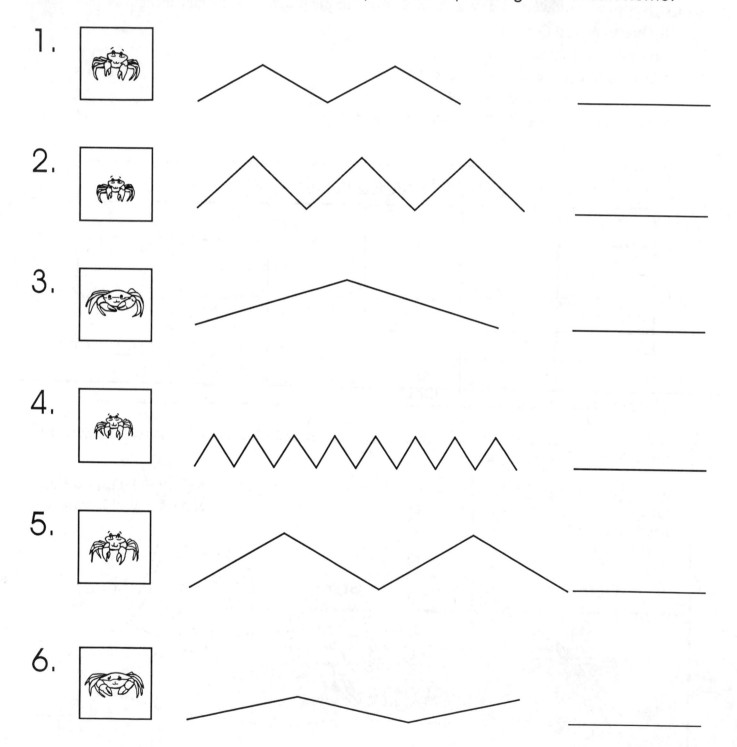

Oil Spill

Many things can destroy a coral reef. They can be destroyed by natural disasters such as hurricanes, and human disasters such as anchor-dragging boats, souvenir collectors, and ocean dumping. Perhaps one of the greatest threats is oil spills. The activity below will allow you to create an oil spill and think of ways to clean it up.

Materials Needed:
- large clear glass bowl
- food coloring (dark color)
- overhead projector
- water
- vegetable oil
- small plastic container
- spoon
- clean-up devices (sponges, cloth, small cups, eye droppers, etc.)

Directions:
1. Set up overhead projector. Fill glass bowl two-thirds with water and place onto projector's viewing area.

2. Place a small amount of oil into the plastic container. Add a few drops of food coloring; mix well with the spoon.

3. Add a few spoonfuls of colored oil to the bowl of water. Discuss what takes place after viewing the projected images. Add another spoonful or two of oil and continue observing.

4. Discuss clean-up of oil spills.

5. Have students create their own oil spills to use in groups, or as a class explore various ways to get rid of the oil. Discuss which methods worked best and why.

6. After students complete this activity, have them invent new ways for removing real oil spills from the Earth's oceans and waterways. They may draw pictures of their inventions as well as write a description of them.

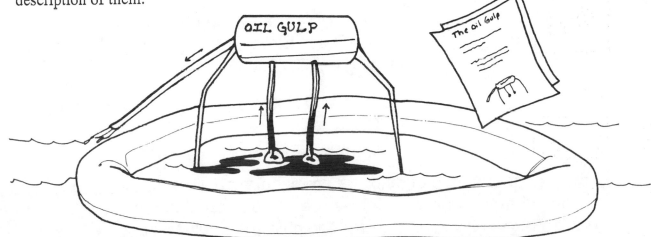

You Can Help!

Today, many of our tide pools and coral reefs are becoming polluted and destroyed due to human carelessness. However, there are things you can do to help save our tide pools, coral reefs, beaches, and oceans.

Pick one or more of the ideas below. When you are finished, tell the class about what you have done and how it has helped our environment. You may have some of your own ideas to add to the list. Share them with others so they can help too!

- When you are at the beach (or park, lake, pond, etc.) take along a biodegradable container and a glove. As you find litter, pick it up and put it in the container; then throw it away (remember to recycle paper, plastic, glass, and cans). Keep track of the kinds of things you find so you can tell the class.

- Sea turtles are an endangered species. If you see one, do not disturb it. Also look out for its eggs which it buries in the sand. Find out about items that are made from sea turtles and do not buy them. You should respect and not disturb any animal you find in nature.

- If you go out on a boat, be very careful to throw away your garbage so that it does not accidentally blow overboard. Dumping things off the boat and into the water can cause animals to get tangled up in these objects or to mistake them for food. Find out why you should cut apart plastic 6-pack rings.

- If you buy helium-filled balloons, dispose of them properly. Balloons released into the air could possibly land in open waters where animals might swallow them. Find out about what might happen if a sea creature swallows a balloon.

- Write to one of the following agencies to find out more information about what you can do to help fight pollution. Share the materials or information with the class.

Center for Marine Conservation
1725 DeSales Street NW
Washington, DC 20036

The Oceanic Society
218 D Street SE
Washington, DC 20003

- Each year, thousands of dolphins are captured and killed by tuna fishermen. Find out what the tuna companies are doing about this problem. Bring in a tuna fish label that has the words "dolphin safe" written on it.

Try This!

Make a Wave

Waves are caused by winds, earthquakes, and the gravitational pull of the moon and sun. Most are produced as wind moves over the water. This causes part of the water to rise. The wind then pushes on the raised water and creates waves. Waves have two main parts—the crest and the trough.

Materials:

- ¹/₂ cup (120 mL) mineral oil
- ¹/₄ cup (60 mL) alcohol
- ¹/₄ cup (60 mL) water
- glass jar with lid
- blue food coloring

Mix ingredients in jar and cover tightly. Slowly move the jar from side to side to make the motion of a wave. Observe the shape.

Can You Make Fresh Water from Salt Water?

Dissolve several tablespoons of salt into a quart (1 L) of tap water. Pour these into small baby food jars for each child. Cover tightly, place in a sunny location, and observe over a few days. Drops of water will form on the underside of the lid. Have each child taste the water. Is it salty? Do you think the water left in the jar is less salty? More salty? Compare what happens to how rain is collected from the ocean. How could we use this information to help people in countries with very few sources of fresh water?

Extension:

Uncover the baby food jars and allow all the water to evaporate.

Taste what is left. What happens to the water?

Float an Egg

Background: Ocean water is heavier than fresh water. Many chemicals are found in the sea. One of those chemicals is sodium chloride (which we use everyday as simple table salt). On the average, the ocean holds about 35 parts salt for every 1,000 parts of sea water.

Fill two glasses with water. Add 2 heaping tablespoons (30 mL) of salt to one glass. Place an egg in each glass. What happens? Why?

Does Water Have Weight?

Background Information: Atmospheric pressure at sea level is almost 15 pounds of pressure per square inch. Oceanographers measure water pressure in atmospheres—one atmosphere = A. In water, every time you go 33 feet (9.9 m) deeper, the weight on your body increases 1 A or another 15 pounds. So at 3,300 feet (990 m), the pressure is measured at 100 A or 1500 pounds of pressure per square inch.

We all understand that solid things have weight. If you lie down flat and place one book on your stomach, you can lie comfortably. But if you piled fifty to one hundred books on yourself, you would be very uncomfortable. If you piled 2,000 books on top of your stomach, you would be squashed flat.

Water also has weight. We can feel comfortable with a certain amount of water on our bodies, such as when we dive to the bottom of a pool, but if we go too deep, we would be squashed flat.

Have students use the Science Experiment Form on page 55 to follow along as you do the experiment, or have students do the experiment in teams.

Question: (What do we want to find out?)

Does water at different levels weigh more or less?

Hypothesis: (What do we think we will find out?)

If I allow water to seep out three separate openings in a can, openings which are spaced vertically and evenly, then the opening at the lowest level will eject the water the farthest.

Procedure: (List step by step)

1. Take one large metal can and drill three evenly-spaced holes down the side.

2. Plug the holes with clay, wax, plumbing tape, or anything that will not allow water to seep through.

3. Place in a large, flattened tray.

4. Fill the container with water.

5. Unplug the holes and observe which hole ejects the water farthest.

Results: (What actually happened?)

The hole at the lowest level ejected the water farthest, while the water from the top opening flowed out more slowly.

Conclusions: (What did we learn?)

More pressure or weight is placed on water at lower levels than on the top levels. Therefore, water pressure changes depending on the depth of the water.

Science Experiment Form

Scientist: _____

Title of Activity _____

Question: What do we want to find out?

_____

_____

_____

Hypothesis: What do we think we will find out?

_____

_____

_____

Procedure: How will we find out? (List step by step.)

1. _____

2. _____

3. _____

4. _____

Results: What actually happened? _____

_____

Conclusions: What did we learn?

_____

_____

Reading a Tide Table

Every day there are two high tides and two low tides. At high tide, the moon's gravitational pull causes the earth's water to rise up on the beaches like a blanket covering the shoreline. This is the time when the tide pool creatures are most active. They do most of their feeding and moving about when under the water. High tide is not a good time to visit the tide pools because the water is so high you will have a hard time seeing anything.

During low tide, the moon's gravity pulls back the water from the beaches, leaving large exposed areas and small pools among the rocks that we call tide pools. This is the best time to visit the beach if you want to see many of the ocean's interesting tide pool creatures.

Some Sunday newspapers print a tide table which tells you when high and low tides will occur. Use the table below to answer the questions about the tides.

High and Low Tides

Day	Time		Time	
Sunday	1:07 a.m.	Low	7:25 p.m.	High
Sunday	1:01 p.m.	Low	7:02 a.m.	High
Monday	1:56 a.m.	Low	8:01 a.m.	High
Monday	1:42 p.m.	Low	8:05 p.m.	High
Tuesday	2:44 a.m.	Low	8:55 a.m.	High
Tuesday	2:22 p.m.	Low	8:38 p.m.	High

Circle T for True or F for False

1. You will see many tide pool animals on Tuesday at 2:44 a.m.   T   F

2. A high tide on Sunday is at 7:25 p.m.   T   F

Fill in the correct times.

3. Monday at _____ is a good time to go to the tide pools.

4. High tides on Tuesday are at _____ and _____.

5. Low tides on Sunday are at _____ and _____.

On the back of this paper, draw pictures of what you would see at the beach at high tide and at low tide.

Charting New Knowledge

In the first column, list all the things you would like to find out about the ocean and animals and plants that live there. As you learn more and more about the ocean and the creatures that inhabit it, use the second column to tell about some of the interesting facts that have amazed and excited you.

What I Want to Learn	Amazing Facts I Am Learning

Tide Pools and Coral Reefs Research Center

Teacher Preparation:

1. Construct your center according to the research center layout diagram on page 59. Remember, your research center may be used year after year, so any time you put into it now—coloring and laminating graphics—will pay off later.

2. Collect reference materials. (See the Bibliography on page 80 for suggestions.) Your school and local libraries are another excellent source of reference materials.

3. Reproduce the map of the world and attach it to the middle section of the center. Also reproduce and attach the research wheel (page 60), animal research sheets (page 62), and the directions for making a diorama (page 63).

Procedure:

Children may work in pairs or in small groups. Plan on using 6 to 10 working periods of 45-60 minutes for the completion of the brainstorming, report writing, and dioramas.

Introduce the center and assign pairings or groupings. Have each pair or group select an animal or island for study.

Research Skills:

Read the Coral Reef Mini Book and Things to Look for in a Tide Pool handouts. As a group, classify on the board the information you are reading according to Looks/Living Habits/Habitat. This gives the children practice in taking notes for research purposes. Have them note that you are writing vital information in incomplete sentences only. Explain that this helps you later when you want to write the information in your own words.

Distribute Brainstorming handout (Animals of the Tide Pools and Coral Reefs, page 62). Have each pair read about the animal or island they have chosen and classify information according to the categories listed.

Reports:

Allow one to two sessions for groups to read their information, list the facts on their brainstorming sheets, and compare results. Once the research is complete, each individual is responsible for writing his/her own research report into a report booklet, complete with illustrations. Distribute copies of the writing paper handouts on page 65.

After reports are written, the group or pair works on final editing of each report.

Presentation:

Distribute the Make a Sensational Sea Diorama handout (page 63). Review the handout with the class. Each child makes his or her own visual display to go with his or her report. Allow two 45-minute sessions or distribute supplies and use as a two-night homework assignment.

Students will present their reports and explain their dioramas to the class. These also make a wonderful display for Open House.

Extension:

Maintain this center during the remainder of your study for extended research. Children can choose other animals to study, and you may choose to assign either extra credit points or to create an incentive program for additional reports (e.g. The Society of Magnificent Marine Biologists).

Tide Pools and Coral Reefs Research Center *(cont.)*

To make this center you will need the following:

3 sheets poster board

2 library card envelopes

report brainstorming sheet

lined paper

paper scraps

shoeboxes

markers

encyclopedias

dictionaries

At this center you will do the following:

1. Research an animal of the tide pools or coral reefs.

    A. Take notes on the brainstorming sheet provided.

    B. Write a 3-paragraph report.

2. Create a visual display (diorama) of your animal and its habitat.

Research Wheel

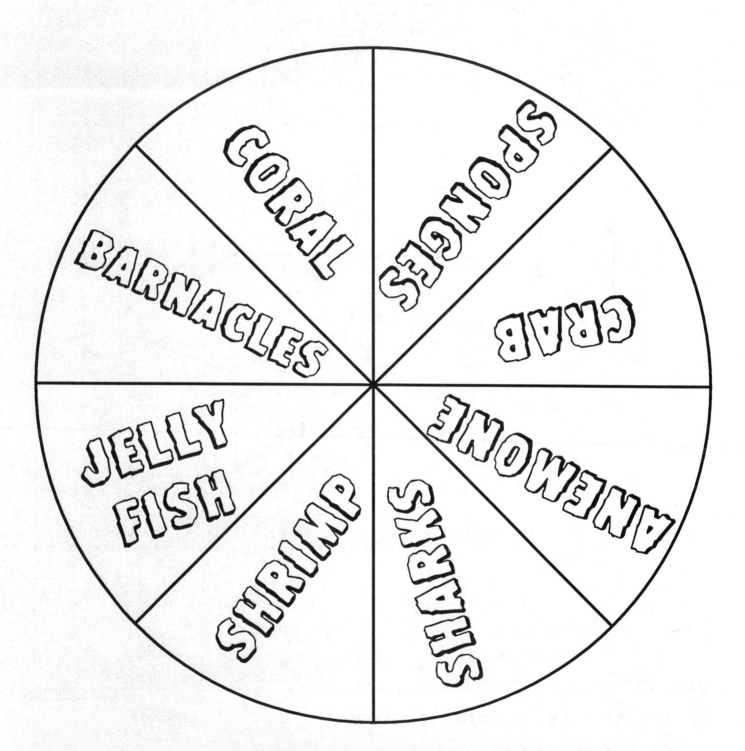

Run off on heavy tag board. Color, cut, and fasten to your research center with a paper fastener.

Research Choices

Below are listings of sea animals that children will enjoy finding out more about on their own.

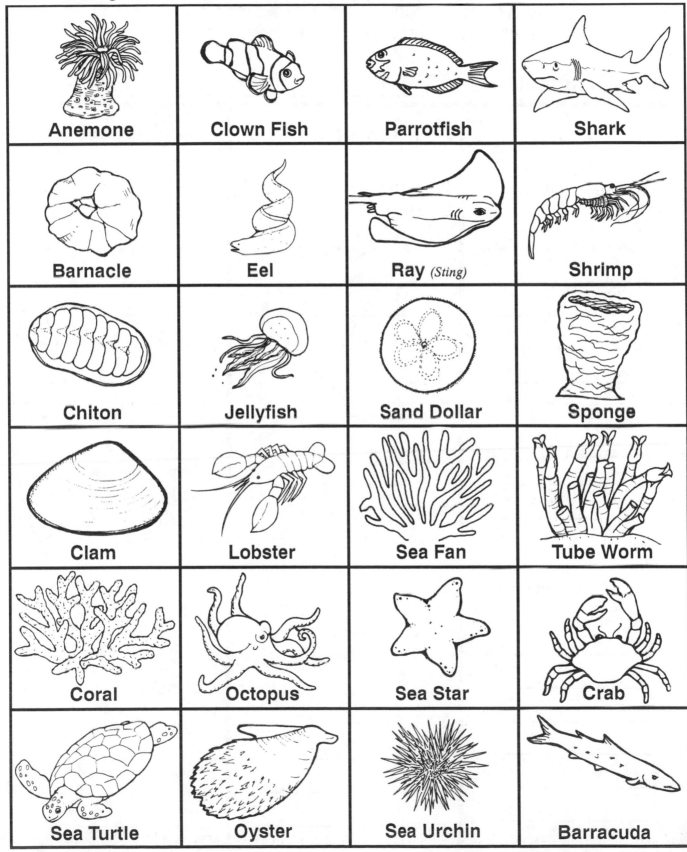

Anemone	**Clown Fish**	**Parrotfish**	**Shark**
Barnacle	**Eel**	**Ray** (Sting)	**Shrimp**
Chiton	**Jellyfish**	**Sand Dollar**	**Sponge**
Clam	**Lobster**	**Sea Fan**	**Tube Worm**
Coral	**Octopus**	**Sea Star**	**Crab**
Sea Turtle	**Oyster**	**Sea Urchin**	**Barracuda**

Animal Research Sheet

Read about your animal in the encyclopedia. Gather information about your animal and list it below. Do not copy in complete sentences but put the information down in your own words. Write three paragraphs, one for each column.

Name of Animal _____

Looks	**Living Habits**	**Habitat**
1. Size (height, length, weight)?	1. How does the animal move about?	1. In which oceans is this animal found?
2. Color(s)?	2. What does the animal eat?	2. In what part of the ocean?
3. Unusual characteristics?	3. How many young does it produce?	3. What problems does this animal encounter in its habitat?
	4. Does this animal live alone or in groups?	
	5. Other information?	

Make a Sensational Sea Diorama

Diorama of an Ocean Habitat

Materials:
- shoeboxes
- construction paper
- tissue paper
- 3-D handout on page 64
- markers
- crayons
- scissors
- glue

Procedure

1. Set up your shoebox. Line the inside with background color using blue construction paper. Now begin creating the floor of your habitat. What is found on the ocean floor? What colors and formations are found in a tide pool? A coral reef?

2. Using various colors of tissue paper and construction paper, illustrate the rest of your animal's habitat.

3. Using the 3-D handout on page 64, draw the animals found in your habitat. Glue these to the different areas of your diorama to show the variety of life in your habitat.

4. Think of what else might be found there. Go to your research material and check to see if there is something else you might like to add.

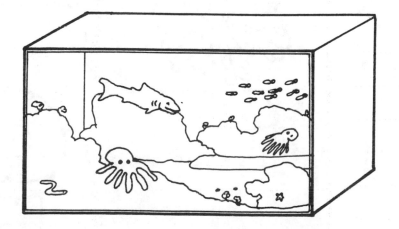

3-D Animals

1. Draw some of the animals on the area above the dotted line. Or, cut out a picture of an animal below and glue it above the dotted line.

2. Cut out the form along the solid line.

3. On the top portion, create a nice look by cutting away the extra paper. Remember to leave the bottom portion attached.

4. Fold under the bottom section and glue to your diorama.

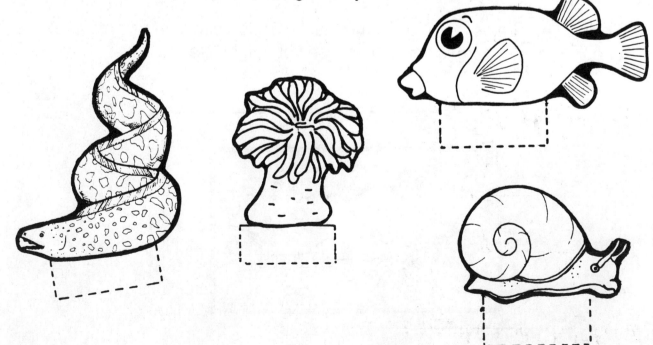

64

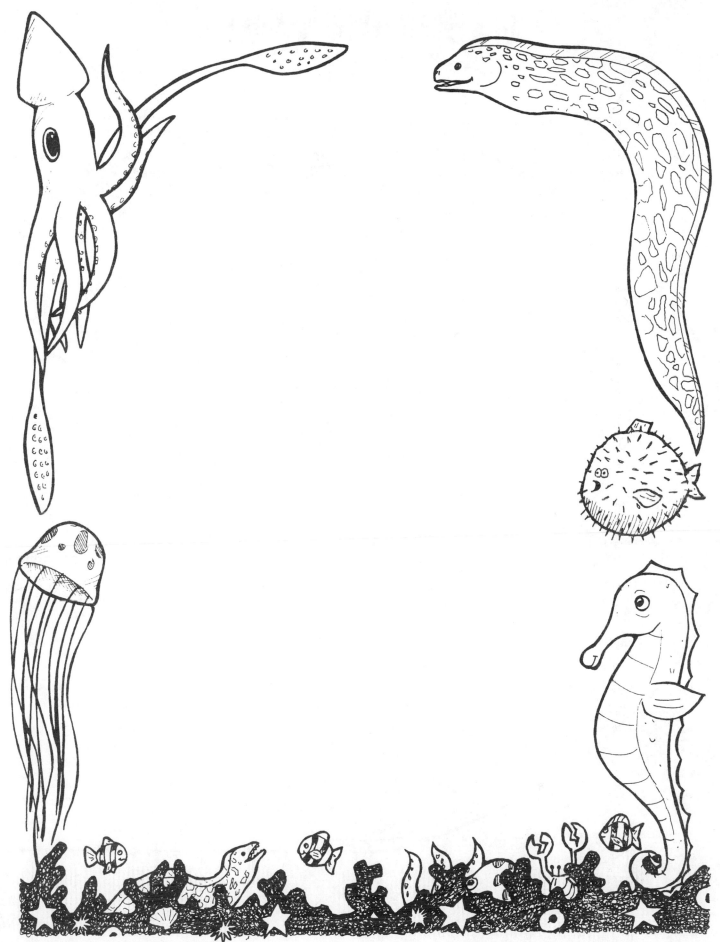

Map of the World

Map of the World (cont.)

T-Shirt

Using the pattern below, design a T-shirt from your coral reef, tide pool, or other sea vacation spot.

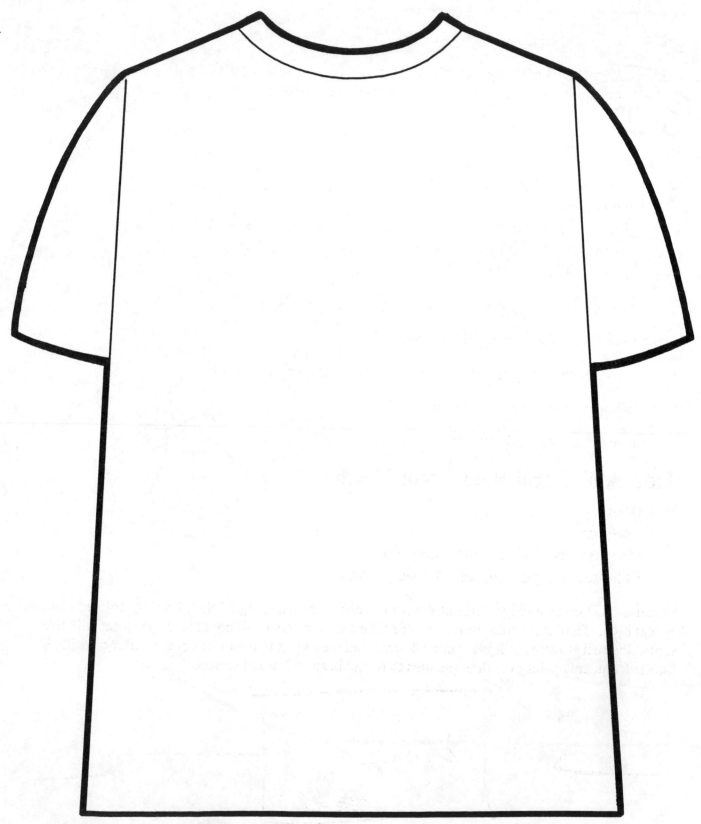

Art Projects

Vacation Travel Brochure

Materials:

- large drawing paper
- samples of travel brochures

Have students fold their paper into thirds, creating a brochure with a cover, a page for things to do on the vacation, and a page for places to see or natural features of their chosen vacation spots.

Sand Painting

Materials:

- large bag of white sand
- food coloring
- plastic food storage bags
- sandpaper squares or construction paper mounted on cardboard
- glue

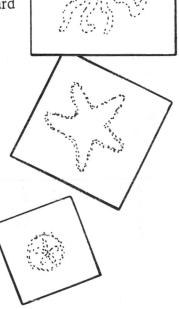

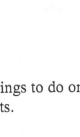

1. Shake several drops of food coloring into plastic bags of sand.

2. Knead until color is evenly distributed.

3. Have students lightly sketch pictures on their sandpaper.

4. Line the pictures with glue and cover with sand.

5. Shake off excess sand and display pictures.

Tide Pool/Coral Reef Color Wash

Materials:

- crayons
- large sheets of white construction paper
- blue tempera paint diluted to a watery solution

Students must color vivid pictures of the coral reef/tide pools, using all their brightly colored crayons except blue. They must color heavily so the blue tempera wash will not adhere to the paper in those spots. Instruct students to leave white all areas that they want to look like ocean. After coloring is finished, students paint over their pictures to reveal beautiful ocean scenes.

Art Projects *(cont.)*

Simple Jellyfish

Materials:

- plastic sandwich bags
- blue, pink, and purple tissue paper cut into 1 inch (2.5 cm) strips
- string

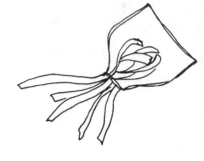

Have each student take a variety of colored tissue paper and place it inside the plastic bag with some streamers hanging out. Then tie the bag with a string.

Paper Plate Crab

Materials:

- paper plates
- red and black crayons
- paper towels
- red construction paper

To make the body, have students fold a paper plate in half and color it completely.

Then direct them to make the arms and legs by cutting eight legs and two claws from red construction paper. These should be glued to the inside cover of the paper plate.

The eyes are made by tearing or cutting a paper towel into fourths and twisting two pieces together for each eye. Flatten the pieces and color eyeballs in center of eye. Then glue them to the middle of the arc of the paper plate, allowing the eyes to hang out over the edge.

Glue the paper plate together.

Fingerprint Tide Pools

Materials:

- various colors of stamp pads
- ink cleanser
- paper towels
- drawing paper
- crayons

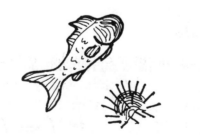

Brainstorm the types of animals found in the tide pools. Think of the shapes of most of these animals. What shapes do they have in common? (circles and ovals) Show children how a fingerprint provides the perfect base for drawing the animals of the tide pools. Instruct children to use all their fingertips to create a variety of sizes to create their tide pool animals. Have students use crayons and markers to finish their rocky tide pool scenes.

Art Projects *(cont.)*

Sea Urchin

Materials:

- clay
- colored toothpicks

Have children form a round shape with the clay. Direct them to insert the toothpicks into the clay.

Pirate Treasure Map

Materials:

- drawing paper
- brown chalk
- tissue
- crayons

Have students carefully tear around the edges of the drawing paper to create an older look to the paper. Using brown chalk, color and smudge the edges. This gives the paper the appearance of being old or slightly burned.

In one corner, have students draw a compass. They may also wish to add a key or a scale.

Brainstorm together on what might be found on a treasure map. Have students create their own maps.

As an extension, have the students do the following writing assignment.

First have students brainstorm the following:

> Where did you find this map?
>
> What did you decide to do with it?
>
> Whom did you take with you?
>
> What happened, and what did you find once you got there?
>
> How did you get back?

Then have children write creative stories about finding their treasure maps.

Drawing Sea Animals

Have students copy the following shapes to create their own sea animals.

Circle
Oval
Triangle
Square
Rectangle
Star

Tide Pool Color by Numbers

1 - yellow   5 - pink
2 - brown   6 - purple
3 - green   7 - blue
4 - red

Let's Sing

"Down by the Sea"

(Sing to the tune of "Down by the Bay," Wee Sing Silly Songs, Price, Stern, Sloan, 1986)

> Down by the sea, where the coral reefs grow,
> Back to the tide pools, I dare not go
> For if I do, my brother will say,
> Did you ever see a turtle wearing a girdle?
> Down by the sea.

Chorus
Other Verse

> Did you ever see a shark who's afraid of the dark?
> Did you ever see a shrimp walk with a limp?
> Did you ever see a barracuda swim to Bermuda?
> Did you ever see a fish making a wish?
> Did you ever see a shell ringing a bell?

"The Twelve Trips to the Tide Pools"

(Sing to the tune of "The Twelve Days of Christmas.")

> On my first trip to the tide pools my true love gave to me, a Northern Yellow Periwinkle.
> On my second trip to the tide pools my true love gave to me two sea slugs and a Northern Yellow Periwinkle.

Continue with the following verses:

    3 rock crabs
    4 star fish
    5 slipper shells
    6 octopuses
    7 sea cucumbers
    8 little mussels
    9 crabs a-pinching
   10 snails a-sliding
   11 urchins lurching
   12 scaled worms

The patterns of the twelve animals from this song can be found on page 74. The patterns have many uses. They can be made into stick puppets and held up as they're mentioned in the song. Students can use the patterns to illustrate a big book of the song. To make a concentration game, copy the page twice and have students color the creatures and cut them out to use as the cards.

Sea Animal Patterns

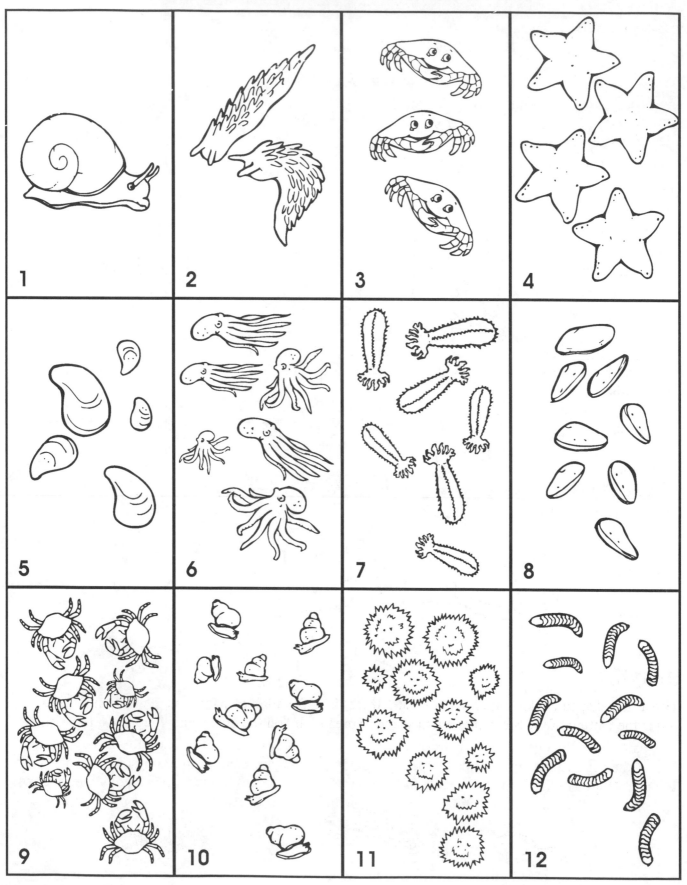

Simple Sea Recipes

Sea Urchin

Ingredients:
- long, thin pretzels
- apple half

Directions:

Stick pretzels into half an apple to resemble a sea urchin. A marshmallow may be substituted for the apple half.

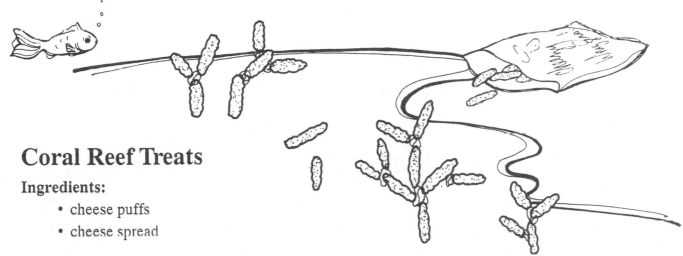

Coral Reef Treats

Ingredients:
- cheese puffs
- cheese spread

Directions:

Stick the cheese puffs together, using the cheese spread as an adhesive. This treat will resemble a coral reef.

Jellyfish

Use a fish-shaped cookie cutter to cut bread. If that is not available, make a cardboard template to guide the cutting of the bread into a fish shape. Spread jelly on the bread, and you have a jellyfish.

Tide Pools and Coral Reefs Festival

As a culminating activity for your unit on tide pools and coral reefs, plan a festival.

- Invite parents and friends. Challenge students to make a haiku invitation. (See page 46.) Send home parent letter provided on page 77 or write your own letter to fit your celebration.

- Before the festival, set up your classroom. Prepare various displays to reflect the unit. Include the research center and dioramas, postcards, salt dough coral reefs, and various art projects.

- You might also have a science station. Have available the equipment and directions of several of the science experiments.

- Display your hermit crab and brine shrimp.

- Have children greet guests at the door.

- Provide entertainment. Children can perform *Hermit Crab* Readers' Theater. The script and various ways of presenting it can be found on pages 13-16. Let children choose which method they would like to use in their presentation. Perhaps it could be done a few different ways by different groups of children.

- Do the limbo and play island music. Students can sing the songs found on page 73 at this time.

- Serve refreshments. Food brings people together. You may want to make some of the food with your class ahead of time or have parents bring all the food. Some simple recipes are suggested on page 75.

- Students can paint a real T-shirt using the design from their shirts on page 68. If you decide to do this, be sure to send a note home early so every student will have a shirt. Some parents may be willing to send an extra one for anyone who does not have a shirt. Some parents may also be willing to donate fabric paint. If these shirts are made ahead of time, they can be worn at the island festival.

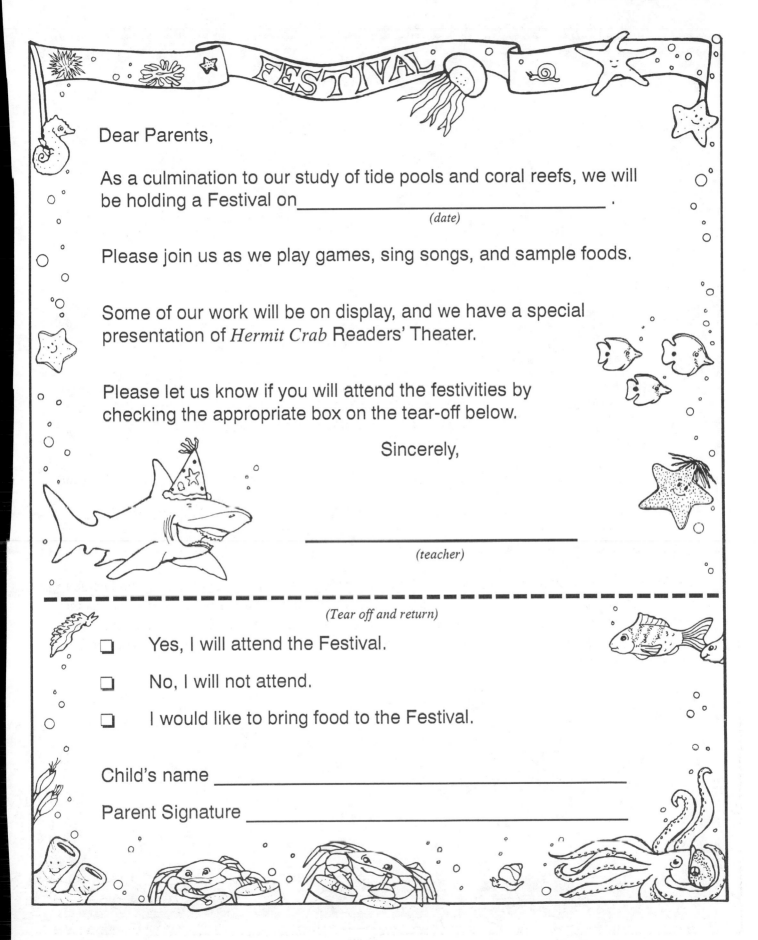

Dear Parents,

As a culmination to our study of tide pools and coral reefs, we will be holding a Festival on_____ .
(date)

Please join us as we play games, sing songs, and sample foods.

Some of our work will be on display, and we have a special presentation of *Hermit Crab* Readers' Theater.

Please let us know if you will attend the festivities by checking the appropriate box on the tear-off below.

Sincerely,

_____
(teacher)

(Tear off and return)

❑   Yes, I will attend the Festival.

❑   No, I will not attend.

❑   I would like to bring food to the Festival.

Child's name _____

Parent Signature _____

Outstanding Oceanographer Award

_____

has effectively completed a course

of study in Tide Pools and Coral Reefs.

Signed,

_____

_____
date

Answer Key

Page 12
1. A jointed body, a shell, and three or more pairs of legs
2. Gills
3. Answers will vary, including crab, shrimp, lobster, barnacle.

Page 21
1. 12
2. 25
3. 24
4. 20
5. 8

Page 27
1. coral reefs
2. polyp
3. tentacles
4. skeletons
5. eggs
6. planula
7. current
8. bacteria

   Bonus: Answers will vary, including sponges, shrimp, urchins, sea fans

Page 32

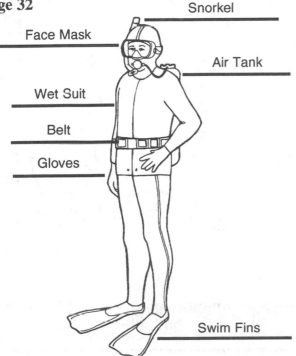

Snorkel

Face Mask

Air Tank

Wet Suit

Belt

Gloves

Swim Fins

Page 35
1. Brain Coral
2. Sea Fans
3. Staghorn Coral
4. Plate Coral

Page 36
1. A
2. B
3. B
4. A
5. A

Page 48
A. 1 pint
B. 1 quart
C. 1 quart
D. 1 gallon or 8 pints or 16 cups
E. 2 quarts or 1/2 gallon or 4 cups
F. 3 pints or 1 quart and 1 pint
G. 2 pints or 4 cups
H. 8 pints or 4 quarts or 16 cups

Bonus
A. 22 cups
B. 24 pints
C. 8 quarts

Page 50
1. 8 cm
2. 12 cm
3. 10 cm
4. 9 cm
5. 12 cm
6. 10 cm

Page 56
1. True
2. True
3. 1:56 a.m. or 1:42 p.m.
4. 8:55 a.m. and 8:38 p.m.
5. 1:07 a.m. and 1:01 p.m.

Bibliography

Nonfiction

Barrett, Norman. *Picture Library Coral Reef.* Franklin Watts, 1991.

The Cousteau Society. *Corals: The Sea's Great Builders.* Simon and Schuster, 1991.

Feeney, Stephanie and Ann Fielding. *Sand to Sea: Marine Life of Hawaii.* University of Hawaii Press, 1989.

Gunzi, Christiane. *Tide Pool.* Dorling Kindersley, Inc., 1992.

Heller, Ruth. *How to Hide an Octopus.* Platt and Munk Publishers, 1992.

Jennings, Terry. *The Young Scientist Investigates: Sea and Seashore.* Children's Press, 1989.

Mainig, Anita. *Where the Waves Break at the Edge of the Sea.* Carolrhoda Books, Inc., 1985.

Morris, Rick. *Mysteries and Marvels of Ocean Life.* Usborne Publishing Ltd., 1989.

Pallota, Jerry. *The Ocean Alphabet Book.* Charlesbridge Publishing, 1986.

Parker, Steve. *Seashore.* Knopf, 1989.

Rotner, Shelley and Ken Kreisler. *Ocean Day.* Macmillan, 1993.

Rydell, Wendy. *All About Islands.* Troll Associates, 1984.

Segaloff, Nat and Paul Erickson. *A Reef Comes to Life.* Watts, 1991.

Taylor, Barbara. *Coral Reef.* Dorling Kindersley, 1991.

Taylor, Kim. *Secret Worlds Hidden Under Water.* Delacorte Press, 1990.

Wood, John Norris and Mark Harrison. *Nature Hide & Seek: Oceans.* Knopf, 1985.

Fiction

Bishop, Claire H. and Kurt Wiese. *The Five Chinese Brothers.* Trumpet Club, 1938.

Hulme, Joy N. *Sea Squares.* Hyperion Books, 1991.

Keats, Ezra Jack. *Maggie and the Pirate.* Scholastic, 1979.

Koch, Michelle. *By the Sea.* Greenwillow, 1991.

MacDonald, Golden and Leonard Wiesgard. *The Little Island.* Doubleday, 1946.

McCloskey, Robert. *Time of Wonder.* Puffin Books, 1985.

McDonald, Megan. *Is This a House for Hermit Crab?* Orchard Books, 1990.

Walton, Rick and Ann. *Something's Fishy! Jokes About Sea Creatures.* Lerner, 1987.

Poetry

Hopkins, L.B., selected by. *The Sea Is Calling Me: Poems.* Harcourt, 1986.

Random House Book of Poetry for Children, "Sea Shell," "The Sea," and "Until I Saw the Sea."

Zolotow, Charlotte. *Everything Glistens and Everything Sings*, "The Sea." Harcourt, 1987.

Music

Nancy Cassidy's *Holler Along Songs: Kids Songs 2*, "Down by the Bay."

Disney's Sebastian, "Under the Sea," "Day-O," and "Jamaica Farewell."

Disney's Sebastian Party Gras, "I'm a Crustacean," "Octopus's Garden," and "Limbo Rock."